The Handbook of BRITISH ARCHITECTURAL STYLES

David N. Durant

First published in Great Britain in 1992 by
Barrie & Jenkins Ltd
20 Vauxhall Bridge Road, London SW1V 2SA

A catalogue record for this book is available from the British
Library

ISBN 0 7126 4862 3 ✓

Designed by: *Carol McCleeve*
Illustrations: © *N. S. Farnell, 1992*
Typeset by *SX Composing*
Printed and bound in Singapore by *Kyodo Printing*

The Handbook of BRITISH ARCHITECTURAL STYLES
David N. Durant

ILLUSTRATIONS BY N. S. FARNELL

BARRIE & JENKINS

LONDON

Contents

Preface

Fashion does not wait for the death of kings neither does it neatly bury a dead style one day and begin another the next. Reading the text of this *Handbook* it should be clear that a fashion dies when patrons tire of it and seek a contrast; but the change is gradual. Take, for example, the heavy and ornate Baroque style, prominent in Britain from the 1660s to *c.* 1725, and which was replaced by the contrasting simplicity of the Palladian style introduced eleven years earlier in 1714. Again, the simplicity of Palladianism was overtaken by Adam's robust neo-Classical style that had some similarities with the earlier Baroque. There will always be revivals of styles. Gothic appeared to be dead until Richard Rogers's Lloyd's building of the 1980s (which employs some Gothic principles in glass and steel instead of glass and stone) and a Palladian Revival of the Rotonda at Vicenza was built in the 1980s in Cheshire by Felix Kelly for Mr Basil Ferranti. It is therefore never safe to say a fashion is dead.

The sections of this *Handbook* are based on styles and the divisions are consequently arbitrary. Furthermore, the lives of architects sometimes span more than one style. In that event I have taken the style in which an architect mainly worked as basis for inclusion in the appropriate section.

All the buildings listed in the gazetteers are accessible to the public except obvious cases such as offices and factories. Before making a visit, it is as well to refer to the current issue of *Historic Houses, Castles and Gardens open to the Public* and check that the property is still accessible or whether written application has to be made. Some buildings mentioned in the text are not open to the public. These are included because they are outstanding examples of an architect's work, but the exteriors will be visible.

Most churches are locked, but with a little local research it is usually possible to find the key-holder.

The architects selected for the short biographical notes are those whose buildings are accessible. Other architects, perhaps of equal influence but none of whose buildings is accessible, are not mentioned. This is a handbook on architectural styles and not a reference book on architects.

Introduction

Architecture is the only art form we can walk into, out of, around and climb over. It is also part of our everyday life, and we have come so used to it that most of us accept what there is: some of it is good, most of the more recent architecture is just plain awful and for so evident an art we deserve something better. It was not always like this. In the eighteenth century an awareness of the rules of architecture was almost universal and opinions were listened to. The result was the creation of façades of elegance and vistas of delight. Were we more knowledgeable today our complaints would carry more weight with planners and architects. I hope this Handbook *will provoke us to demand better architectural standards.*

The Greeks invented classical architecture in the sixth century BC. It was based on the simple post and lintel construction used in timber buildings, that is, upright posts supporting cross beams. The Romans carried this further and worked out perfect proportions for the uprights and decorative details for the capitals, the architrave, frieze and cornice (the top of the columns and the divisions of the horizontal beam). It was still post-and-lintel architecture. The Romans also invented the semi-circular arch that did away with the lintel.

After the end of Roman civilization, the Normans (Norsemen who had settled in Normandy) used the Roman arch in their Norman or Romanesque architecture. By the twelfth century Romanesque had developed into early Gothic architecture. This 'Gothic' architecture has nothing to do with the Goths who had defeated the Romans; it is used as term of reference. The principles of Gothic architecture evolved in northern Europe around the invention of the pointed arch, leading on to stone ribbed vaulting, an alternative to the post-and-lintel principle.

Architecture is a matter of construction and both classical and Gothic evolved out of the use of stone for building. Timber was used for buildings throughout these centuries, but the advanced principles used in stone construction have no application in timber construction, which continued the old post-and-lintel principle, progressing to the rigid timber-frame.

Until new building materials were discovered, Gothic and classical were the only architectural styles used in European buildings. Classical is distinguished by symmetry and Gothic by asymmetry. There were fashions for the one or the other through the centuries, fashions exploited by clever architects sensing a need for change. From about 1530 the architectural style was classical in one form or another until the nineteenth century when an historical trend brought in a Gothic Revival. The styles used in the classical period have been given distinguishing names such as Elizabethan (1558-1603) and Baroque, the style in fashion from, say, 1660 to 1720. Throughout this essentially classical period the Gothic style continued in use, principally in church architecture, and some buildings, such as the Houses of Parliament, rebuilt after a fire in 1834, are classical in concept (i.e. symmetrical) but Gothic in decoration.

In the nineteenth century two new methods of building were developed: steel-framed and reinforced-concrete constructions. The first steel-framed building was the Home Insurance Building, Chicago, USA, by Jenney in 1883-5. Concrete reinforced with steel rods under tension, although a French invention of 1849, was not used in a building until 1870. With these two new building methods architects could at last break free from the old choices of Gothic or classical.

With hindsight changes in architectural style are easily explained, but for the architects of any given period it is not so easy to see the direction fashion may take. Clearly, an overblown style filled with what was termed 'movement', such as the Baroque, must be followed by a plain style, and Baroque was indeed followed by the Palladian Classical. This plainer style in its turn gave way to the neo-classical that again employed 'movement' (i.e. advancing and receding exterior walls with fussy classical decoration). This neo-classical style was superseded by the plain and simple Greek Revival of the early nineteenth century which was itself eclipsed by a return to the complicated Gothic Revival.

Successful architects anticipate changes of fashion, as did Robert Adam (1728-92) when he introduced the neo-classical style in the 1760s. Not all were so lucky; Colen Campbell (1673-1729) correctly anticipated Palladianism as early as 1714, but it took the patronage of Lord Burlington (1694-1753) to make the style fashionable from 1725 when architects other than Campbell exploited the new architectural taste.

The architecture of the nineteenth century appears to many to be something of a maze, but unlike earlier eras the Victorians knew and said exactly what they were doing. First, they jettisoned what they saw as 'foreign' sources – the Roman and Greek classical styles – replacing these with what they believed to be English architecture. They were not particularly clear about the historical truth and took Gothic and Tudor to be truly English. Of course they were wrong; Gothic was in the main inspired from France and Tudor decoration was a mixture of Gothic and Netherlandish Renaissance. By the 1870s Gothic was looking very much overplayed and there was yet another return to earlier plainer styles when even Adam had a revival before the end of the century. The main drive of architectural inspiration came from the Arts and Crafts movement in the discovery of traditional rural architecture. It seems by chance that the Victorians discovered a truly British style, still evident today in the long rows of suburban houses with mock-Tudor timbering and leaded lights.

Glossary

ABACUS: Flat slab at the top of a capital.

AMBULATORY: Polygonal or semicircular aisle enclosing an apse; originally used for processions.

APSE: Polygonal or semicircular vaulted termination, usually in a chancel or side chapel.

ARCADE: Series of arches carried on columns or piers.

ARCHITRAVE: Lowest of the three parts of an entablature. Also the surround of a window or door.

ASHLAR: Smooth faced masonry.

ATTIC: A building's top storey when its height is less than that of the others.

BAILEY: Courtyard of a castle.

BARBICAN: Outwork defending a castle entrance.

BARGEBOARDS: Decorated or plain boards on a gable end covering the ends of the horizontal roof timbers.

BATTLEMENT or **CRENELLATION**: Parapet with high and low portions called respectively merlons and embrasures.

BEAKHEAD: Norman ornament consisting of mythical birds' and beasts' heads with long pointed beaks. Believed to represent Norman masks.

BLOCK CAPITAL: Cube shaped Romanesque capital with rounded lower angles.

BUTTRESS: Projecting brickwork or masonry giving support to a wall.

CANTILEVER: Horizontal projection with no visible support.

CAPITAL: Head of a column.

CHANCEL: The east end of a church containing the altar.

CHOIR: Usually in the chancel where devine service is sung.

CLERESTORY: Windows in upper storey of walls lighting a church or hall.

CRUCK: Curved timber supporting both roof and walls.

DAIS: Raised platform at one end of a medieval hall.

DECORATED: Historical division of Gothic architecture from 1300 to 1350.

DORMER: Vertical roof window.

EARLY ENGLISH: Historical division of Gothic architecture from late C12 to late C13.

ELEVATION: The face or plane of a building.

ENGAGED COLUMN: Part-column attached to a wall.

ENTABLATURE: The whole horizontal and decorated member supported by a classical column, composed of architrave, frieze and cornice.

GIANT ORDER: Classical column rising from ground level through several storeys.

GIBBS SURROUND: Alternating large and small blocks of stone surrounding a door or window.

HA-HA: Sunk fence or wall bounding a park or garden.

HOOD-MOULD: Projecting ledge over a door or window to throw off water.

IMPOST: Projection on which the end of an arch rests.

LANCET WINDOW: Narrow pointed-arched window.

LIERNE: Vault rib springing from the side of an other rib; C14.

LINTEL: Horizontal beam over an opening.

MOTTE-AND-BAILEY: Primitive castle consisting of a *motte* (or earth mound) with a wooden tower on it, surrounded by a ditch and palisade, the bailey.

MULLION: Vertical upright of wood or stone in a window.

NOGGING: Brickwork filling the spaces between wall timbers.

ORDERS: Classical column in one of Doric, Tuscan, Ionic, Corinthian or Composite style.

ORIEL: Bay window on an upper floor.

PARAPET: A low wall high up on a building.

PEDIMENT: Gable over a classical portico, window or door.

PERDENDICULAR: Historical division of Gothic architecture from c. 1360 to 1525.

PIANO NOBILE: Principal floor of a house with main rooms of reception.

PIER: Solid masonry support of any kind, not a column.

PILASTER: Shallow rectangular column attached to a wall.

PINNACLE: Decorative termination of a spire or buttress angle.

PORTICO: Covered centre-piece over entrance of a house, temple or church often supported on attached and detached columns.

PURLIN: Horizontal roof timber resting on the principal rafters.

RENDERING: Cement or plaster covering of a wall.

ROMANESQUE: The style of architecture of the C7 to C12 including Anglo-Saxon and Norman.

RUSTICATION: 'Rock-faced' unfinished surfaces of stonework.

SCREENS PASSAGE: Screened passage at the entrance of lower end of a great hall with doors to services.

SOLAR: Any upper room of a house. Not a term used in this book and definitely not an alternative for a Great Chamber.

STIFF-LEAF: Early English carved decoration of many lobed leaves.

STRAPWORK: Decoration of interwoven bands taken from embroidery designs; common in C16.

TIERCERONS: Secondary vaulting-rib springing from one of the main springers, or from a boss, to the ridge-rib; later C13.

TRANSEPT: Transverse arm in a cruciform church.

TRANSOM: Horizontal bar of stone or wood in a window.

VAULT: Continuously arched ceiling or roof.

VENETIAN WINDOW: Three-light window of which the centre light is arched and widest. English fashion of C17 and C18.

WATER-LEAF: Carved leaf-shape used in later C12 capitals.

ABBREVIATIONS

Att. = Attributed.
Aug. = Augustinian.
Ben. = Benedictine.
CC = County Council.
Cist. = Cistercian.
DC = District Council.
EH = English Heritage.
HBM = Historic Buildings and Monuments.
Hos. = Hospital.
Mon. = Monastery.
NT = National Trust.
Nun. = Nunnery
NTS = National Trust for Scotland.
Premon. = Premonstratensian.
Sec. = Secular.
SSS = Secretary of State for Scotland.
Vic.Soc. = Victorian Society.
WHM = Welsh Historic Monuments.
WNT = Welsh National Trust.

THE ROMANESQUE ERA

ROMANESQUE 600-1200

Romanesque is the term used to denote the architectural style of the period from the end of the Roman Empire in the sixth century to the development of the Gothic c.1200. It applies to the entire area of western Europe between Scandinavia and Italy, from lowland Scotland to Germany. In Britain, 'Romanesque' embraces both the Saxon and the Norman styles.

The remains of Roman architecture are still evident in Britain in the old cities founded by the Romans, such as York, Leicester and Exeter. The builders used an enduring method of stone or brick construction based on the round arch, an extremely strong and characteristic feature. However, the 'Dark Ages' intervened between the departure of the Romans from Britain c.400 and the arrival of the Normans in 1066. They brought with them a style of architecture developed from that of the Romans. The intervening 600 years were not without architectural innovation.

Saxon mercenaries from north-west Germany, whom the Romanised Britons had invited to help defend them against Scottish raiders, turned on their hosts c.420. It was no more than they deserved since they too had plundered and raided in south-eastern England after the withdrawal of Roman law and order. From 450 the Saxons began settling in southern and central England.

They constructed their dwellings of timber and consequently nothing has survived above ground. But enough can be discovered from excavations to show that the Saxons introduced the distinctive 'open hall' house constructed of whole or split logs standing upright. Simply one large room open to the rafters, with a fire burning on a central hearth, the open hall house was the perfect answer to feeding and accommodating large numbers of people. So convenient, in fact, that the 'hall' remained in common use in British dwellings for 1000 years and has been a continuous feature in the colleges of Oxford and Cambridge from their foundation down to the present day. The Saxons were also responsible for what became a national style of church building in stone. The number of complete Saxon churches is small and other churches, understandably, contain only fragments of Saxon work set in walls of later periods.

Christianity virtually disappeared from Britain from the time of the Romans until the sixth century. The earliest Christian building in Britain may be represented by the walls of the Casa Candida at Whithorn (Dumfries and Galloway), built c.400 by St Ninian, a Romano-British bishop. Christianity was brought from Celtic Ireland to Scotland by St Columba in 563 and evidence of three of his missionary bases exist, the first on Iona itself, his second on a remote island to its south, Eilach-an-Naoimh, and another small monastic complex at Chaluim Chille on Skye, now exposed in the dried-out bed of a loch.

While the Celtic Church in Scotland extended its mission as far as Northumberland, in the south Christianity was served directly from Rome. In 597 St Augustine became the first Archbishop of Canterbury. The site of his monastery is outside the walls of the city at the bottom of St Martin's hill. The earliest Anglo-Saxon work in the south, predating St. Augustine, is to be found in the reused Roman brickwork in the north wall of the chancel of St Martin's, Canterbury.

From 800 Anglo-Saxon England suffered raids from the Vikings of Norway and Denmark. Some of these raiders settled in England and established villages still to be distinguished by their suffix 'by'. The Vikings also lived in timber open halls, although nothing remains above ground today. Northern France was also raided and settled by the same Norsemen who later invaded England under William I with an army of under 10,000 men in 1066. The Bayeaux tapestry shows his defeated opponent Harold, before the battle of Hastings, feasting in an upper-hall of his palace at Bosham.

A detail from the Bayeux Tapestry: King Harold feasting in a Saxon upper-hall at his palace at Bosham, West Sussex.

Of this palace nothing remains, but at Boothby Pagnell in Lincolnshire there is a well-preserved example of a Norman upper-hall in what was a prosperous manor house of *c*.1200. Beneath the hall is a vaulted undercroft originally used for storage. Other than a surrounding moat to deter outlaw gangs, Boothby Pagnell had no defences. The Normans did, however, build nearly forty castles in England (some on older Roman and Anglo-Saxon sites) as defence against local insurrection. Most were built of earth and timber but all were of the motte-and-bailey type. The *motte* (Norman-French for a mound) was surrounded by a bailey, an enclosure defended by a ditch or ditches and a palisaded rampart. The castles were easily and quickly constructed of local materials and needed no masons or quarrymen. In the 150 years following the Conquest some 3,000 timber castles were built.

The building of stone castles in England began some twelve years after the Conquest. They did not develop from the earth and timber motte-and-bailey but were copied directly from prototypes in Normandy. The plan was similar and consisted of a central strongpoint, the *donjon*, with a surrounding bailey. The best known example is the Tower of London with a four-storey hall-keep. The White Tower was completed in 1079 and contains a hall with royal apartments and private chapel on the top third floor; the fourth storey was added later.

SAXON CHURCHES

Surprisingly, one timber Saxon church, dating from at the latest *c*.1013, survives in the nave of St Andrew at Greensted, Essex, but drastically restored in the nineteenth century. No doubt, there were many more. Two other timber churches in Essex, at West Hanningfield and Stock, have characteristic late Saxon plans although both date from the fourteenth century. Otherwise, there are some 400 churches with visible Saxon stonework. The finest, undoubtedly, is at Brixworth, Northamptonshire. Built *c*.680 by monks from Peterborough, it was intended to be impressive. The apse was destroyed by Vikings and rebuilt *c*.1000 when the porch was built upwards to form the present tower. The loveliest is St Mary's at Deerhurst, Gloucestershire, built *c*.790, twice destroyed by Vikings, rebuilt *c*.930 and altered *c*.1030, when the present tower was added. Nearby is the tiny St. Odda's chapel, built 1053-6, completely preserved but forming part of a half-timbered farmhouse.

The Celtic Christian churches of St Columba in the north were built with rectangular chancels, while those of the Roman Christian mission of St. Augustine in the south were built with apsidal east ends derived, as one might expect, from the Roman basilica or meeting hall.

Typical Features of Saxon Churches

Plan: Sited east-west (although unusually, St Laurence, Bradford-on-Avon is sited ENE) and rectangular in the north of Britain but with an apsed chancel in the south. Towers at the west end were added after *c*.1000. The cruciform plan with central tower over the transept is represented by St Mary's, Stow, Lincolnshire, the largest to survive, built *c*.1010 but ruined by the nineteenth century and rebuilt. The aisled nave with a smaller plain chancel is very rare.

St Andrew's, Greensted, Essex. The only surviving timber Saxon church c.1013. Restored in the nineteenth century when the dormers were inserted.

Materials: Apart from the one surviving timber church at Greensted, Essex, usually built of rough stone of irregular shape. Cut stone (ashlar) except for buttresses, window and door openings, is very rare. The exterior was usually rendered. Few stone churches were built earlier than forty years before the Conquest. On Roman sites, tiles and bricks were reused.

Roofing: No original Saxon examples survive, but most were thatched; some towers – Rhenish helm, saddle-back or cruciform – are roofed with oak shingles.

Elevation: High walls with small openings using Roman semi-circular arches or triangular architraves with imposts. External window splays are a certain Saxon feature. Other distinctive features are the building of corners in 'long and short work' (large stones set alternately upright and horizontal) and the use of narrow, squared pilaster strips, an example of the translation of timber into stone. Later churches have stonework laid herring-bone fashion.

SAXON CHURCH TOWERS

*Above. 'Renish Helm steeple at
Sompting, West Sussex'.
Centre. 'A saddle-back tower'.
Below. Cruciform at Breamore,
Hampshire.*

Above. A Saxon window showing typical 'imposts' supporting a straight-sided arch.

Opposite. The west tower at Earl's Barton, Northamptonshire, c.1020 with typical Saxon detail of 'long-and-short work' at the corners and narrow pilaster strips.

Interiors: Dark and high.

Where to See Examples
North – **Barton-on-Humber**, Humberside, c.950, tower c.990; **Broughton**, Humberside, tower c.1000; **Bolam**, Northumberland, tower c.1050, church Norman; **Corbridge**, Northumberland, tower c.780 & c.1030; **St John's**, Escomb, County Durham, complete and small, c.680; **Heddon-on-the-Wall**, Northumberland, nave and chancel c.1020-50; **Hexham**, Northumberland, crypt c.680; **St Patrick's Chapel**, Heysham, Lancashire, c.800; **Kirkdale**, North Yorkshire, nave tower arch and chancel arch c.1060; **Kirk Hammerton**, North Yorkshire, c.1050, 'done over' in late-C19th; **Ledsham**, West Yorkshire, 800-1050, Norman tower; **Monkwearmouth**, Sunderland, Tyne and Wear, tower of two dates c.675 & c.1000; **Morland**, Cumbria, base of tower c.1060; **Norton**, Cleveland, tower and transepts c.990; **Ripon**, North Yorkshire, crypt c.670; **St Mary Bishophill Junior**, York, tower c.1020-60.
Midlands – **Barrow**, Shropshire, chancel and arch c.1040-50, rest Norman c.1100; **Brixworth**, Northamptonshire, c.680; St Peter-de-Merton, **Bedford**, Bedfordshire, tower of c. 1000; **Carlton-in-**

Lindrick, Nottinghamshire, tower *c.* 1000 & 1050; **Clapham**, Bedfordshire, Anglo-Danish tower; **Earl's Barton**, Northamptonshire, tower *c.*1020; St Michael's, **St Albans,** Hertfordshire, nave and chancel *c.*950; St Wystan, **Repton,** Derbyshire, *c.*760-870; **Stow**, Lincolnshire, huge church *c.*1010; All Saints, **Wing**, Buckinghamshire, nave and chancel 700s, rebuilt *c.*950.

East – **Barnack**, Cambridgeshire, tower of *c.*1020; **Dunham Magna**, Norfolk, nave *c.* 1040; **Forncett St Peter**, Norfolk, tower *c.*1020-60; **Great Paxton**, Cambridgeshire, magnificent interior *c.* 1020, central tower; St Bene't's, **Cambridge**, tower and arch *c.*1040.

South – **Arlington**, East Sussex, Saxon nave, Norman chapel; **Boarhunt**, Hampshire, complete small church *c.*1060; **Bosham**, W. Sussex, *c.*1040-50; **Bradford-on-Avon**, Wiltshire, quite small, one of the best, early 700s, central tower; **Bradwell-juxta-Mare**, Essex, *c.*640; **Breamore**, Hampshire, *c.*1010; **Canford Magna**, Dorset, chancel & nave *c.*1000; Holy Trinity, **Colchester,** Saxon west tower with original timbers *c.*1020-40; **Coln Rogers**, Gloucestershire, nave & chancel *c.*1030; St Mary's, **Deerhurst**, Gloucestershire, *c.*700 and tower of *c.*1020, perhaps the best; Earl Odda's Chapel, **Deerhurst,** Gloucestershire, 1056; St Mary in Castro, **Dover,** Kent, all of *c.*1000 but over-restored in 1841, central tower; St Piran-in-Sablo, **Newquay**, Cornwall *c.*500-700; **Ford**, West Sussex, *c.*1060s; **Knowlton**, Dorset, ruined, *c.*1020; **Little Bardfield**, Essex, nave & tower *c.*1000; **Old Shoreham**, West Sussex, north wall with blocked door; St Mary's, **Sompting**, West Sussex, 'Rhenish helm steeple' *c.*1040-60; **Strethall**, Essex, nave *c.*1060; **Thorington**, Suffolk, round tower *c.*1060; St Nicholas, **Worth,** West Sussex, *c.*1030-50; **Wickham**, Berkshire, tower *c.*1020.

Scotland – **Birsay**, Orkney, largely ruined, *c.*1050; **Brechin**, Tayside, round tower, 990-1012; **Eilach-an-Naoimh**, Inner Hebrides, remains of St Columba's 2nd monastery, *c.*700-900.

NORMAN CASTLES

After the Conquest William I gave Saxon properties to 150 of his leading supporters and barons. However, to prevent too much power accumulating in one area, the holdings were spread over several counties. He also gave one quarter of all land to the Church and kept one-fifth for the Crown. These estates were protected by the building of thousands of simple motte-and-bailey castles. Many of these were later replaced by more permanent shell-keeps in stone: Totnes in Devon represents a motte-and-bailey of *c.*1070, rebuilt as a shell-keep in stone *c.*1200. At Windsor Castle, the Round Tower (which is not in fact completely round) was built *c.*1150 as a shell-keep.

The king and the great barons whom he installed in troubled areas (the Welsh Marches and East Anglia) built more ambitious hall-keep castles. These were for living in and had, inevitably, impressive great halls. At Hedingham Castle, Essex, the keep, built *c.*1130, gives a very good impression of the style in which these magnates

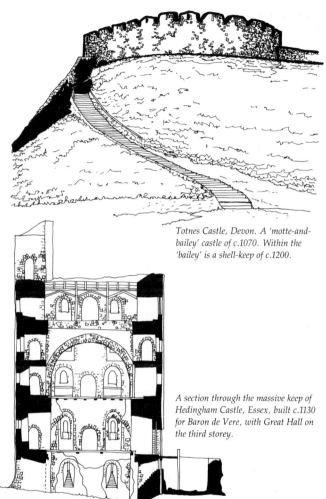

Totnes Castle, Devon. A 'motte-and-bailey' castle of c.1070. Within the 'bailey' is a shell-keep of c.1200.

A section through the massive keep of Hedingham Castle, Essex, built c.1130 for Baron de Vere, with Great Hall on the third storey.

lived. The prototypes of such huge castles were in Normandy: rectangular and multi-storeyed with the principal apartments on the upper floors. The forbidding bulk of the keep of Rochester Castle, Kent, built for the Archbishop of Canterbury c.1130 by Gundulph, the Norman Bishop of Rochester and his masons, is a notable example. He also built the White Tower of London and the massive, but unfinished, hall-keep at Colchester c.1080.

A castle therefore can be of three types: the shell-keep and the hall-keep (both with a surrounding curtain wall) and the later high curtain-wall with no keep. A hall-keep could be rectangular, round, polygonal or oval, depending on the whim of the builder and the nature of the site. From the beginning, the Norman kings meticulously controlled castle building by licence. About 1000 were built up to the reign of Stephen in 1135. Thereafter, in the twenty years of anarchy marking his reign, perhaps a further 1000 were built without licence. A castle was an expression of feudal power and it controlled the local population within a radius of some ten miles. Early castles were purely military but, as time passed, other factors controlled their design. Rich landowners keen to display their wealth and power demanded higher standards of living than were offered by the bleak early stone halls. And so began the conflicting demands of domesticity and defence. The interior of Conisbrough Castle, Yorkshire, for example, built by Henry II's half-brother c.1180, was very different from that of Richmond Castle in the same county.

The first two Crusades to the Holy Land (1095-9 and 1147-8) offered an opportunity to test castle design to the limit and so had an important influence on military defence. Concentric defensive walls, such as those at Dover Castle built c.1180-90, can only be a direct result of this experience.

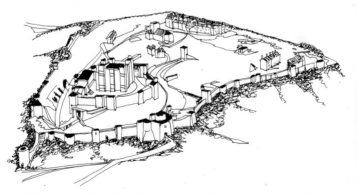

Bird's-eye-view of Dover Castle. The square keep in the centre was built from 1170 by Henry II, the outer circling walls were built c.1200 and based on experience gained on the Crusades.

Typical Features of Norman Castles
Plan: Shell-keep; round or oval, open centre with battlemented gallery on wall tops, surrounded by a curtain wall enclosing a bailey. Accommodation was provided by wooden structures within the walls of the keep and against the curtain walls. Hall-keep: rect-

angular, round, oval or polygonal, multi-storied with basement for storage, guard-room on ground floor, two-storeyed great hall above and principal chambers with chapel on upper floors. Orford Castle, Suffolk, of which only the keep remains was a royal castle built 1165-1173 for Henry II which strangely has no upper chambers at all.

Elevation: Shell-keeps had stone walls, rough coursed (or occasionally ashlar) up to 32ft in height and up to 10ft thick and thicker at the base. Windows, small, round-arched on upper floors, defensive arrow slits on lower floors, with a single entrance. The hall-keep had walls 15ft thick and *c*. 90ft in height. The hall-keep entrance was often above ground level.

Where to See Examples

North – _Alnwick_ (D. of Northumberland), Northumberland, shell-keep *c*.1150, restored C14, C18, & C19; **_Appleby_**, Cumbria, square hall-keep *c*.1180, restored in C17; **_Bamburgh_**, Northumberland, square hall-keep *c*.1130-50; **_Bowes_** (EH), North Yorkshire, rectangular hall-keep *c*.1171-90; **_Brougham_** (EH), Cumbria, rectangular hall-keep *c*.1180; **_Conisbrough_** (EH), South Yorkshire, polygonal hall-keep *c*.1180; **_Middleham_** (EH), North Yorkshire, rectangular keep and curtain walls *c*.1170; **_Norham_** (EH), Northumberland, square hall-keep *c*.1160, 2 upper floors added C15; **_Pickering_** (EH), North Yorkshire, tower and hall *c*.1180 but shell-keep C13; **_Prudhoe_** (EH), Northumberland, rectangular hall-keep and gatehouse *c*.1150; **_Richmond_** (EH), North Yorkshire, rectangular hall-keep *c*.1150-80,

Section through the polygonal keep of Orford Castle, Suffolk, built 1165-73 for Henry II. The basement, used for storage, is beneath the lower hall and the Great Hall is on the third storey. There are no bedchambers.

and Scolland's Hall 1st floor hall and some curtain walls *c*.1090; **Scarborough** (EH), North Yorkshire, square hall-keep and curtain wall, 1158-68; **Tickhill**, South Yorkshire, gatehouse, curtain walls *c*.1180.

Midlands – **Kenilworth** (EH), Warwickshire, square hall-keep, *c*.1170; **Ludlow**, Shropshire, gatehouse and inner bailey walls *c*.1110; **Newark** (Newark & Sherwood DC), Nottinghamshire, gatehouse, chapel and SW tower *c*.1180; **Oakham**, Leicestershire, only hall survives *c*.1180-1200; **Snodhill Castle**, Peterchurch, Hereford and Worcester, ruined polygonal hall-keep on motte *c*.1190; **Peveril** (EH) Derbyshire, square keep, curtain wall *c*.1080; **Tamworth**, Staffordshire, shell-keep *c*.1180.

East – **Bungay,** Suffolk, square hall-keep *c*.1140; **Castle Acre** (EH), Norfolk, oval shell-keep with hall-tower inside *c*.1190 on earlier earth motte-and-bailey *c*.1080; **Framlingham** (EH), Suffolk, high curtain wall *c*.1190-1210, experimental design influenced by Crusades; **Norwich** (Norwich CC), Norfolk, rectangular hall-keep *c*.1160; **Orford** (EH), Suffolk, polygonal hall-keep 1165-73, restored by Salvin (q.v.) 1833.

South – **Arundel** (Arundel Cast. Trust), East Sussex, motte *c*.1080s, shell-keep *c*.1170s, restored 1791 & 1890; **Berkhamstead** (EH), Hertfordshire, motte-and-bailey *c*.1160; **Castle Hedingham**, Essex, square hall-keep *c*.1130 on earlier motte; **Carisbrooke** (EH), Isle of Wight, polygonal shell-keep and curtain wall *c*.1160. C12 great hall; **Chilham** (Vt. Masserene & Ferrard), Kent, polygonal great-tower *c*.1171; **Colchester**, Essex, rectangular hall-keep *c*.1080; **Corfe**, Dorset, square hall-keep *c*.1110-20, with bailey wall; **Eynsford** (EH), Kent, rectangular hall-keep *c*.1140, flint curtain wall *c*.1090; **Lewes**, East Sussex, remains of oval shell-keep and gatehouse *c*.1100; **Tower of London** (Hist. Roy. Palaces), rectangular hall-keep *c*.1078-97; **Pevensey** (EH), East Sussex, square hall-keep *c*.1100; **Porchester** (EH), Hampshire, square hall-keep *c*.1120; **Rochester** (EH), Kent, square hall-keep 1127; **Windsor** (HM the Queen), Berkshire, motte *c*.1087, shell-keep *c*.1080, upper floors C19.

South West – **Launceston** (EH), Cornwall, round shell-keep *c*.1200 with later high round tower inside; **Restormel** (EH), Cornwall, oval shell-keep *c*.1200; **Totnes** (EH), Devon, round shell-keep *c*.1200 on motte with bailey *c*.1100.

Scotland – **Castle Roy**, Highland Region, quadrangular curtain-wall *c*.1200; **Castle Sween**, Strathclyde Region, quadrangular shell-keep *c*.1200.

Wales – **Bridgend** (WHM), Mid-Glamorgan, curtain-wall, *c*.1190; **Bronllys** (WHM), Powys, motte-and-bailey *c*.1100, round hall-keep *c*.1200; **Cardiff** (Cardiff CC), South Glamorgan, 12 sided shell-keep *c*.1200 on motte *c*.1080; **Dolbadarn** (WHM), Gwynedd, round hall-keep *c*.1200 curtain wall *c*.1100s; **Dolwyddelan** (WHM), Gwynedd, small square hall-keep *c*.1190; **Manorbier** (WHM), Dyfed, gatehouse and hall-keep *c*.1140; **Ogmore** (WHM), Mid-Glamorgan, rectangular hall-keep *c*.1140-50; **Skenfrith** (WNT), Gwent, round hall-keep *c*.1200 on earlier motte.

NORMAN HOUSES

The majority of wealthy Normans preferred to live in the safety of castles, and few houses survive. Of these most have first-floor halls and all are late Norman when it had become safer to live in undefended dwellings. The famous 'Jew's House' at Lincoln was more probably the house of a rich merchant. Its hall is above ground-floor store rooms, but the original doorway, windows and chimney-breast survive. The more important dwellings had a chamber off the hall, but usually all the occupants would have slept in the hall round a central hearth. At Boothby Pagnell Manor, Lincolnshire, a late-Norman building (*c*.1200), the hall has a canopied hearth on a side wall, and the chamber is unheated. Windows were small with round-arch architraves and decoration was used sparingly. Pele-towers are defensive towers typical of the Scottish borders. They consisted of an undercroft with hall over and a chamber above the hall.

Where to See Examples
North – *Bridekirk*, Cumbria, Dovenby Hall pele-tower *c*.1200; *Burton Agnes*, Humberside, *c*.1170; *Pendragon Castle*, Mallerstang,

The 'Jew's House', Lincoln, c.1710-80. A merchant's house with first floor hall, two romanesque windows and original chimney breast over the original entrance. The ground floor, now shops, was for storage.

Cumbria, one of the first pele-towers (q.v.) *c*.1200, badly ruined; **Sinnington**, North Yorkshire, barn was manor hall *c*.1190.
Midlands – Boothby Pagnell, Lincolnshire, *c*.1190-1200; **Lincoln**, Lincolnshire, 'Jew's House' *c*.1170-80, 'Norman House' *c*.1170-80, St Mary's Guild *c*.1180-90.

The Old Manor, Boothby Pagnell, Lincolnshire. A late Norman (c.1190-1200) first floor hall, with chamber lit by a two-light Norman window and storage on the ground floor, originally moated.

East – Bury St Edmunds, 'Moyses Hall' *c*.1180; **Cambridge**, 'School of Pythagoras', *c*.1190; **Hemingford Grey**, Cambridgeshire, *c*.1180; **Norwich**, 'Music House' undercroft only survives *c*.1175.
South – Blisland, Devon, Manor·House *c*.1190; **Canterbury**, Eastbridge Hospital *c*.1180-90; **Iford**, East Sussex, Swanborough Manor, *c*.1200; **Horton**, Avon, priest's house of *c*.1170-80; **Portslade**, East Sussex, ruined remains late 1100s; **Saltford**, Avon, *c*.1150; **Southampton**, Hampshire, 'Merchant's House' *c*.1150, 'Long House' (ruins) *c*.1180, remains of dwellings in town walls; **Westdean**, Charleston Manor, *c*.1170-80; **West Malling**, Kent, shell of small house *c*.1150.

NORMAN CATHEDRALS

At the time of the Norman invasion there were twenty Anglo-Saxon dioceses each with its own cathedral. Of these thirteen were refounded under the Normans and rebuilt. Other sees were created and others moved. Between 1090 and 1100 work was in progress on no fewer than thirty-two cathedral, abbey and priority sites. The Normans undertook this huge programme of building for three reasons: they were reforming the old Saxon church; they regarded Saxon architecture as outmoded; and a council held at Windsor in 1072 decreed that rural sees should be moved to a major town in the diocese. Selsey went to Chichester, and the diocese with its see at Donchester-on-Thames, was shifted to Lincoln, leaving Dorchester to become an abbey. In Norfolk there were two moves: the first from the old Saxon see of North Elmham (where the ruins of *c*.1000 are to the north of the parish church) to Thetford, and finally to Norwich where the cathedral was begun in 1096. Henry I created Ely and Carlisle cathedrals and rebuilt Peterborough, which only became a cathedral in 1541. Of the thirteen original Anglo-Saxon cathedrals rebuilt by the Normans many have evidence of Saxon work incorporated in the fabric. In Scotland David I (1124-53) founded Dunblane Cathedral *c*.1130, and began St Magnus's, Kirkwall, Orkney, in 1137.

Together with the secular cathedrals there were cathedral priories, unique to Britain, and cathedral monasteries. These were mainly Benedictine, while Carlisle, Dorchester, Hexham and St Germans were Augustinian foundations of the twelfth century. From the north of England, devastated by William's army, came the most original innovations. York, begun in 1080, differed from all other Anglo-Norman cathedrals at the time in having no aisles, so necessitating a huge timber roof-span of 45 ft, and the central crossing covered an unprecedented area of 2,000 sq. ft. Durham was equally adventurous in that the architect used a system of ribbed, stone vaulting for the first time with a span of 39 ft across the nave, a design which must have been conceived in the 1090s, although the cathedral was not consecrated until 1133. Both York and Durham are important because they foreshadowed what was to follow in the thirteenth century: the all-stone church, the flying buttress and the pointed arch.

The examples of York and Durham took a long time to be digested and it was only in the later twelfth century that the Gothic style began to develop in England. This is best seen in the choir at Canterbury (1175) showing the transition from Norman to Gothic.

Typical Features of Norman Cathedrals, Abbeys, etc.

The hallmarks of Norman architecture are the round arch (inherited from the Romans but used more robustly than by the Saxons with their smaller openings), the long nave (demanded by the clergy), the crossing tower and two towers at the west end. The use of the thick-wall technique resulted in walls of immense width (at Durham they are 9ft). In early buildings the piers are equally huge (at Durham they have a radius of 10ft) but by the second half of the twelfth century the coming of Early English is foreshadowed by lighter piers. Decoration on arches and cornices consisted of billet, chevron, zigzag (from *c*.1110), rope and human and mythical animal heads and, almost unique to Britain, cushion capitals.

Plan: Cruciform with long aisled nave and short choir.

Elevation: Three storeyed (nave arcade, triforium and clerestory), larger windows with semi-circular heads, blind arcading on towers and shallow buttresses.

Interior: Early Norman work used massive drum piers succeeded later by lighter piers decorated with columns and cushion capitals. Stained glass from *c*.1180 at Canterbury and York, paving at Byland Abbey of the same date.

The nave of Durham Cathedral built c.1200 with the first Gothic stone vaulting.

A detail of the choir of Canterbury Cathedral, rebuilt after a fire in 1174 and showing the transition from Norman round arches in the clerestory and triforium to the Gothic pointed arches below.

DETAILS OF ROMANESQUE DECORATION

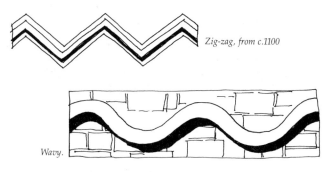

Zig-zag, from c.1100

Wavy.

Round Billet, 1130s.

Pellet, 1130s.

Cable, 1140s.

Nail head.

Hatched.

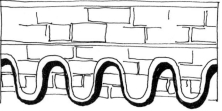

Nebule.

A Corbel table.

Lozenge.

Cushion capital.

Animal head.

Blind arcading at Much Wenlock Priory, Shropshire, c.1080.

Where to See Examples

North – *Carlisle* (Sec. & Aug. Abbey), Cumbria, crossing and transept 1130-60; *Cartmel* (Aug. Priory), Cumbria, church *c*.1190-1220; *Durham* (Ben.), Co. Durham, choir, presbytery and nave 1093-1137; *Kirkstall Abbey* (Cist. Abbey), West Yorkshire, impressive ruins, *c*.1155-75; *Selby* (Ben. Abbey), North Yorkshire, nave and transepts *c*.1100-80; *York* (Sec.), North Yorkshire, crypt *c*.1070.

Midlands – *Abbey Dore* (Cist. Mon), Hereford & Worcester, chancel, crossing and transepts *c*.1180-1210; *Blyth* (Ben. Priory), Nottinghamshire, nave *c*.1090; *Croyland* (Ben. Abbey), Crowland, Lincolnshire, south aisle façade and other remnants *c*.1114-90; *Dorchester* (Sec. & Aug.), Oxfordshire, fragments of presbytery and transept *c*.1180; *Freiston* (Ben. Priory), Lincolnshire, nave and crossing arch *c*.1120-80; *Gloucester* (Sec. & Ben. Mon.), Gloucestershire, crypt, ambulatory, nave and chapter house *c*.1090-1120; *Hereford* (Sec.), Hereford & Worcester, nave, transept and eastern arm *c*.1110-45; *Haughmond* (Aug. Abbey), Shropshire, chapter house, entrance and refectory *c*.1160-70; *Lincoln* (Sec.), Lincolnshire, lower parts of west front *c*.1075; *Southwell* (Sec. Minster), Nottinghamshire, west front (except window), nave, transepts *c*.1120-50; *Tewkesbury* (Ben. Abbey), Gloucestershire, nave, crossing, west front (except window) *c*.1087-1150; *Worcester* (Ben.), Hereford & Worcester, crypt and south chancel chapel 1080s; *Worksop* (Aug. Priory), Nottinghamshire, east front, towers and nave *c*.1140-1200.

East – *Bury St Edmunds* (Ben. Abbey), Suffolk, gatehouse and ruins 1081-1140; *Binham* (Ben. Mon.), Norfolk, nave *c*.1130; *Ely* (Ben.), Cambridgeshire, transept, nave *c*.1100-40, west front & tower *c*.1150, Prior's door *c*.1160; *Norwich* (Ben.), Norfolk, chancel, transepts nave & west front 1110-1145; *Peterborough* (Ben. Abbey), Cambridgeshire, choir, transepts and nave, 1118-90; *St Albans* (Ben. Abbey), Hertfordshire, all but complete of 1077-88 in Roman brick from Verulamium; *Waltham Holy Cross* (Aug. Abbey), Essex, nave *c*.1120.

South – *Canterbury* (Ben. Mon.), Kent, fragments 1070-7 in transept and eastern arm; *Chichester* (Sec.), West Sussex, choir, nave, transepts 1090-1184, clerestory 1190+; *Christchurch* (Aug. Priory), Hampshire, crypt, transepts and crossing *c*.1095-1130; *Exeter* (Sec.), Devon, transept, transept towers *c*.1170; *Ford Abbey (Cist. Mon.), Dorset,* chapter house *c*.1150; *Dover*, Kent, Refectory of St Martin's Priory *c*.1140; Christ Church (Aug. Abbey), Tom Quad, *Oxford*, chapter house entrance, lower parts of nave, tower and crossing *c*.1130-1185; *Rochester* (Ben. Mon.), west front & nave *c*.1150; *Romsey* (Ben. Nun.), Hampshire, nave, crossing and transepts 1120-1200; St Cross (Hos.), *Winchester*, Hampshire, complete church *c*.1190; *Wimborne Minster* (Sec.), Dorset, crossing and nave *c*.1170; *Winchester* (Ben. Mon.), Hampshire, crypt, north & south transepts *c*. 1070-80.

Scotland – *Dryburgh Abbey* (Premon. Abbey), Borders Region, west front, chapter house and cloister buildings *c*.1150-90; *Dunblane*, Central Region, founded by David I, *c*.1130, only tower survives; **Dunfermline** (Ben. Mon.), Fife Region, nave c.1128-50; **Kelso** (Ben. Abbey), Borders Region, remains of church c.1180-1200; **Kirkwall**, Orkney, c.1137-80.

Wales – St David's (Sec.), Dyfed, nave c.1190-1200; **Llantony** (Aug. Mon.), Gwent, famous ruins c.1175-1230; **Margam** (Cist. Abbey), West Glamorgan, nave and west front 1150-90; **Penmon** (Priory), Anglesey, church c.1120-70.

NORMAN CHURCHES

The early buildings are indistinguishable from those of the Saxon period (Saxon masons were, after all, still being used) and it is difficult to give firm dates. However, the early churches were small with apsed chancels and good examples of these are found in Surrey at Farleigh, Pyrford and Wisley, and in Sussex at Buncton, Hardham and Stopham. The chapel in the White Tower, (Tower of London c.1078-97) is a brilliant example of the management of spaces; a single area of apse and nave is surrounded by an ambulatory with gallery above. Most Norman churches built after c.1130 had increasing use of decoration. By the end of the twelfth century the style was moving into the Gothic of Early English and this can be seen at St Cross Hospital church, Winchester, where both pointed and round arches are used with skill and intricate carving decorates slender columns – very different from the heavy masonry of the early Norman work.

Typical Features of Norman Churches

Plan: Early Norman has short unaisled naves and apsed chancels. From c.1130 naves are longer and aisled with square chancels. A few circular churches survive based on the plan of the Holy Sepulchre, Jerusalem; examples are the Temple Church, London, St. Sepulchre, Northampton, St Sepulchre, Cambridge, a roofless chapel at Ludlow Castle and the remnants of a circular plan at Orphir, Mainland Orkney.

Elevation: Massive stonework, tall, narrow, round-arched windows becoming wider and highly decorated later. The huge drumpiers of the early years give way to lighter piers decorated with attached shafts.

Decoration: From c.1100 the well-known zigzag motif and the billet decorations around windows, doors, arches and string courses appear, becoming more complex later. From c.1130 sculpted, ornate capitals become more common. Beakhead is more common after c.1140. By c.1170 complex intersecting arcading appears, porches, previously few, become more common, pointed arches appear and by c.1180 the familiar zigzag has developed into a key or chain pattern. Wall-paintings survive in several Sussex churches.

Useful Dates

c.1110: Zigzag decoration (consisting of a series of Vs) is introduced.
1130s: Zigzag becomes common with billet, reel and pellet, scal-

Left. Beakhead after c.1140
Above: Late-twelfth century 'Water-leaf' capital.

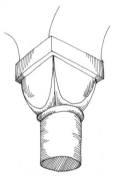

Left. 'Before c.1160s the Abacus (the stone at the top of the column) was square'.
Above. 'After c.1160s the Abacus became polygonal or round'.

loped, voluted, and sculpted capitals and blind arcading.

1140s: Foliage carving becomes more complex and beakhead, diaper, rosettes and cable decorations are introduced; bell capitals introduced by Cistercian monks.

1150s: Multi-order doorways appear; beakheads take animal faces.

1160s: Zigzag carving becomes three dimensional; the abacus becomes round or polygonal instead of square or rectangular.

1170s: Porches become common and the pointed arch begins to be used, water-leaf (sculpted leaves) introduced.

1180s: The zigzag sometimes becomes key and chain-patterns.

Where to See Examples

North – **Adel**, West Yorkshire, almost complete *c.*1160; **Aldingham**, Cumbria, nave *c.*1190; **Barton-le-Street**, North Yorkshire, *c.*1160; **Birkin**, North Yorkshire, almost complete *c.*1160; **Edlingham**, Northumberland, nave, chancel arch and porch *c*.1180, tower a little later; **Felixkirk**, North Yorkshire, apsed chancel and nave *c*.1130-40, over-restored C19; **Healaugh**, North Yorkshire, tower nave and chancel *c*.1140-80; **Hornby**, North Yorkshire, tower, chancel and N arcade *c*. 1080-1180; **Long Marton**, Cumbria, mix of early Saxon/Norman and late Norman, tower and chancel *c*.1070-1190; **Old Berwick**, Northumberland, *c*.1120; **Pittington**, County Durham, spectacular arcade *c*.1115-20; **St Bees**, Cumbria, Benedictine nunnery church *c*.1160; **Thockrington**, Northumberland, *c*.1100; **Warkworth**, Northumberland, long nave and chancel *c*.1100, tower 1200; **Weaverthorpe**, Humberside, tower, nave and chancel *c*.1110.

Midlands – **Astley**, Hereford & Worcester, nave *c*.1160; **Berkswell**, West Midlands, almost complete *c*.1180; **Bishop's Cleeve**, Gloucestershire, nave and crossing *c*.1160-90; **Boothby Pagnell**, Lincolnshire, nave and tower *c*.1140-80; **Cassington**, Oxfordshire, nave lower part of tower *c*.1120; **Coln St Dennis**, Gloucestershire, nave, chancel and central tower *c*.1140; **Corley**, Warwickshire, nave and chancel arch *c*.1110-70; **Deeping St James**, Lincolnshire, nave of Benedictine monastery church *c*.1190; Heath Chapel, **Diddlebury**, Shropshire, perfectly preserved *c*.1130-60; **Dunstable**, Bedfordshire, priory church *c*.1130-60; **Dymock**, Gloucestershire, *c*.1100-40; **Edstaston**, Shropshire, nave and chancel all *c*.1180; **Elkeston**, Gloucestershire, outstanding *c*.1170; **Kempley**, Gloucestershire, tunnel-vaulted chancel *c*.1100 with paintings of *c*.1180; **Kilpeck**, Hereford and Worcester, complete with apsed chancel *c*.1140-50; **Leominster**, Hereford and Worcester, priory church, nave, 1121-*c*.1150; **Littleborough**, Nottinghamshire, *c*.1070-80; **Mathon**, Hereford and Worcester, nave *c*.1070, chancel *c*.1160; **Melbourne**, Derbyshire, large and all of *c*.1135-50, except apse rebuilt C14; **Moccas**, Hereford and Worcester, almost complete *c*. 1110-20; **Morcott**, Leicestershire, interior mainly *c*.1110; Holy Sepulchre, **Northampton**, modelled on Holy Sepulchre, Jerusalem, *c*.1120; St Peter, **Northampton**, *c*.1150-60; **Ifley**, Oxford, completely of *c*.1170, restored 1856; **Peterchurch**, Hereford and Worcester, *c*.1120-30; **Prestbury**, Cheshire, interior altered but of *c*.1160; **Rock**, Hereford and Worcester, mainly *c*. 1170; **Rudford**, Gloucestershire, *c*.1120; **Ryton-on-Dunsmore**, Warwickshire, nave and chancel *c*.1090; **Sookholme**, Nottinghamshire, small, pre-1100; **Steetly**, Derbyshire, small, nave, apsed chancel, *c*.1100-50; **Stewkley**, Buckinghamshire, *c*.1140-50; **Stoneleigh**, Warwickshire, nave and chancel arch *c*.1120-30; **Swyncombe**, Oxfordshire, small, nave and apsed chancel *c*. 1080, altered 1850; **Tarrington**, Hereford and Worcester, nave and chancel *c*.1130; **Whaplode**, Lincolnshire, nave and chancel arch *c*.1180-90; **Wyken**, West Midlands, almost complete *c*.1120.

East – St Mary Magdelene, **Barnwell**, Cambridge, leper chapel, nave, chancel *c*.1150; **Copford**, Essex, complete with paintings *c*.1150-80; **Easthorpe**, Essex, *c*.1130; **Hales**, Norfolk, nave, chancel and tower *c*.1150; **Heckingham**, Norfolk, nave, apsed chancel, round tower *c*.1150; **Ickleton**, Cambridgeshire, nave and crossing *c*.1100; *Isleham*, Cambridgeshire, priory church, nave and apsed chancel *c*.1090; *Kirby Crane*, Norfolk, chancel and nave *c*.1180; Saxon tower *c*.1020; *Tilney All Saints*, Norfolk, nave and chancel *c*.1180-90 roof and tower later; *Walsoken*, Norfolk, *c*.1180-90, tower later; *Wymondham*, Norfolk, abbey church nave *c*.1130.

South – *Avington*, Berkshire, almost complete *c*.1160; *Barfreston*, Kent, nave and chancel *c*.1190; *Bere Regis*, Dorset, nave *c*.1160-80; *Canford Magna*, Dorset, tower, nave *c*.1170; *Chatham*, Kent, chapel of St Bartholomew's Hospital *c*.1130, restored C19; *Chipping Ongar*, Essex, almost complete *c*.1100; *Chobham*, Surrey, nave and chapel *c*.1100-80; *Compton*, Surrey, *c*.1180; *Compton Martin*, Somerset, nave and chancel *c*.1120-30; *Culbone*, Somerset, mainly Norman; St John, *Devizes*, Wiltshire, *c*.1100-60; *East Barnet*, Hertfordshire, early Norman nave; *East Meon*, Hampshire, cruciform plan *c*.1150; *Farleigh*, Surrey, nave and chancel, *c*.1100; St Mary, *Guildford*, Surrey, crossing arches, nave and 2 chapels *c*.1100-80; *Hadleigh*, Essex, complete church with apsed chancel *c*.1140; *Hardham*, West Sussex, nave and chancel *c*.1080s, faded wall paintings *c*.1130; *Hemel Hempstead*, Hertfordshire, tower, nave, crossing and chancel *c*.1140-80; *Icklesham*, East Sussex, tower, nave and chapels *c*.1100-1200; *Iford*, East Sussex, tower, nave and chancel *c*.1200; St Anne, *Lewes*, East Sussex, tower, nave and 1 transept but much altered *c*.1190; St John's Chapel, The Tower, *London*, *c*.1090; Temple Church, *London*, WC2., modelled on Holy Sepulchre, Jerusalem, round, *c*.1130; *Lullington*, Somerset, *c*.1150; St John the Baptist, *Margate*, Kent, chancel and long nave *c*.1140; *North Marden*, West Sussex, tiny with apsed nave *c*.1090; *Patrixbourne*, Kent, small *c*.1180, restored 1857; *Pentlow*, Essex, nave and apsed chancel *c*.1100; *Polstead*, Suffolk, earliest English brick arches, nave and chancel *c*.1170s; *Pyrford*, Surrey, nave and chancel *c*.1100; St Aldhelm's Chapel, *Gt Aldhelm's Head*, Dorset, tiny chapel *c*.1180; *Selham*, West Sussex, nave and chancel *c*.1070s; *New Shoreham*, West Sussex, towers, transepts and chancel *c*.1130-90; *Smeeth*, Kent, nave and chancel *c*.1120, chapel *c*.1200; *Steyning*, West Sussex, *c*.1160-80, chancel 1863; *Stogursey*, Somerset, *c*.1100-80; *Stoke-sub-Hamdon*, Somerset, *c*.1130-40; *Stopham*, West Sussex, nave and chancel *c*.1070s; *Stoughton*, West Sussex, cruciform. *c*.1080s; *Studland*, Dorset, *c*.1090-1120; *Sutton*, Kent, nave and chancel *c*.1120; *Sutton Bingham*, Somerset, small *c*.1070-1160; *Warnforth*, Hampshire, *c*.1180-1200; *Winchfield*, Hampshire, *c*.1170; *Winterborne Tomson*, Dorset, tiny *c*.1090; *Witley*, Surrey, nave, chancel and wall paintings *c*.1180.

Scotland – *Birnie*, Grampian Region, nave and apse *c*.1120-50; *Dalmeny*, Lothian Region, nave, chancel and apse *c*.1150-60; *Duddingston Church*, Edinburgh, mainly Norman; *Edinburgh*, Queen Margaret's Chapel in the Castle, *c*.1180; St Magnus, *Egilsay*, Orkney, chancel, crossing and nave *c*.1110; St Rule's Church, *St Andrews*, Fife Region, *c*.1140.

Wales – *Ewenny Priory Church*, Mid-Glamorgan, complete *c*.1140; *St Clears*, Dyfed, long nave *c*.1110-20.

THE GOTHIC ERA

Medieval Gothic 1200-1530

The term 'Gothic' has nothing to do with the sacking of Rome in 410 by the barbarian Goths. But it does mean the splendid soaring architecture of the 'Dark Ages', a time when earlier historians imagined Europe to be overrun by hordes of savage and uncivilized Gothic tribes. 'Gothic' came to denote an art that is not classical, that is to say is neither Greek nor Roman.

Good architecture is a matter of proportion, control of spaces and solid forms, while decoration is of secondary importance. The Romans understood this and it was not a discipline really rediscovered until the church architecture of the medieval period.

Gothic church architecture is characterised by ribbed vaulting, the pointed arch and the flying buttress. To understand these engineering features it helps, when looking at a Gothic building, to image the stresses on the structure caused by weight thrusting down on the foundations and how these stresses are directed around windows and doors and carried over spaces by vaults. The foundations of a building carry the weight of the structure above it. A plain blank wall creates no structural problems provided it is vertical; when a hole is made for a door or a window the strength of the wall is weakened. To counteract this weakness the weight of the wall directly above an opening is transferred down its jambs, or sides.

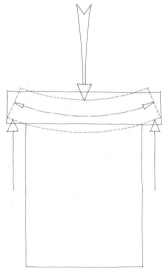

The lintel carries the weight of the wall above. Stone is strongest under compression and has been wrongly used in this example – it does not transfer the stress to the jambs at the side and will fracture.

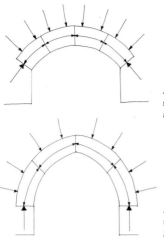

A shallow arch transfers stress sideways and needs thick walls to hold it.

A Gothic pointed arch transfers stress vertically downwards so allowing lighter walls.

Norman builders bridged their openings with strong semi-circular arches carried on walls of immense thickness. In fact, a semicircular arch creates more horizontal stresses than a pointed arch: the Romans were using the least safe of arches and that is why Roman walls are so thick. An acute-angled arch directs more thrust downwards than a wider-angled arch in which more thrust is directed sideways. It has been said that complete verticality would result in complete safety; complete horizontality would burst the two walls apart at once. Lighter walls can be used provided the weight is transferred vertically and, as we have seen, by 1200 cathedral builders were experimenting with the pointed arch.

A pitched roof on a building tends to force its load-bearing walls outwards unless the roof is correctly constructed. In this respect, a flat roof is no structural problem: its weight is carried directly downwards by the walls. But a sharply pointed roof, like an acute-angled arch, puts an outward thrust on the walls that carry it. There are various ways of constructing this type of roof to reduce these pressures but in principle the problem remains. The solution was found with the 'flying buttress' which applies a counterbalancing horizontal thrust at the exact point where it is needed whereby the thrust is transferred downwards through its own arch. Until architects found the right formula for the flying buttress there were undoubtedly some very nasty accidents.

Other serious accidents were caused by central towers being carried on inefficiently engineered arches. The crossing had to be free of columns to give the congregation a clear view of the priest conducting the service. This resulted in the necessity to have very wide

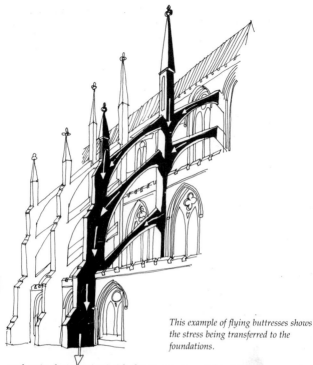

This example of flying buttresses shows the stress being transferred to the foundations.

arches in the crossing with the immense weight of the tower carried on four load-bearing piers. Poor foundations beneath a crossing pier or insufficient buttressing resulted in collapse – the most frequent accident to befall cathedrals. Eight central towers have collapsed: St David's (1220), Lincoln (1237) and Ely (1322), earlier central towers fell at Abingdon (1091), Winchester (1107) and, during a remodelling of an earlier tower, at Beverley c.1200. Later, Selby Abbey's tower collapsed in 1690, and Chichester's central tower fell as recently as 1861. The insertion of 'strainer arches' in the central crossing of Wells, soon after the tower was completed in 1322, undoubtedly prevented another collapse. The nineteenth-century architect, Sir George Gilbert Scott (1811-78), later saved the towers of St David's and St Albans cathedrals by strengthening the supports.

Rib vaulting was no more than the principle of the pointed arch applied to the Romanesque barrel vault. The thrust of a barrel vault is continuous and requires a continuous abutment for stability, but the thrust of a Gothic vault, the intersections of which are reinforced with ribs, is dispersed along the ribs to 'collection points' at intervals along the walls.

These three developments, the pointed arch, rib vaulting and the flying buttress, created the possibility of soaring height, vast window spaces and amazingly complicated systems of stone vaulting over naves and choirs, and all were taken advantage of and developed to the maximum by the end of the medieval period.

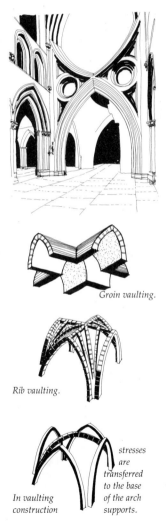

The insertion of 'Strainer arches' at Wells Cathedral in 1322, prevented the collapse of the crossing tower.

Groin vaulting.

Rib vaulting.

In vaulting construction stresses are transferred to the base of the arch supports.

King's College chapel, Cambridge, fan vaulting c.1480.

However, it was not the architects who called the tune in cathedral building but the demands of the priests who devised church ritual. They required long naves with aisles for processions, ambulatories in the choir, also for processing, and longer chancels. The apsed chancels of Norman cathedrals were rebuilt longer and with a rectangular east end. Liturgically, the choir was of greatest importance and this was where rebuilding usually started – even if it proceeded no further, as was the case at Southwell in 1234-41. The earliest rebuilding of an outmoded Norman choir was at Hereford (c.1190); this was followed by Lincoln (1192). A total of sixteen choirs were rebuilt including Llandaff (1193), Brecon and Chester (1194), Hexham and Lichfield (c.1195), Rochester (c.1200), Wimborne and Winchester (1202), Pershore (c.1210), Southwark (c.1212), Beverley (c.1220), Worcester (1224) and Ely ((1239). The cost of all this must have been huge, indicating the importance attached to the choir.

Although the structural elements of Gothic architecture were devised in England, the artistic element emerged in the Ile-de-France at the time of the Capetian ascendancy. One of the best examples is in the Abbey church at St Denis, near Paris, begun in 1140, where the effect inside is of lightness, of supple curves and energetic concentration. The anonymous architect who designed the choir of St Denis can be said to have invented the Gothic style. His invention was soon taken up across the Channel in England; Wells is the first truly English Gothic cathedral begun about forty years after the St Denis Abbey church.

However, the Gothic style was never static and for convenience historians have separated the 330 years of the medieval period into style groups; the first 100 years, to 1300, is called Early English, although the first cathedrals to use this style were Wells and Lincoln, both built at the end of the previous century. By comparison with what was to follow this could be called the 'horizontal' style. In the nave of Lincoln one's eye follows the strongly marked horizontal string courses below the arches of the triforium and clerestory. The following period, Decorated, which is self explanatory, ran for some fifty years to 1350 and refers exclusively to decoration; traceried windows, ogee or double-S curves in arches and maximum decoration covering surfaces all of which were likely to have been brightly painted. The east end of Wells (c.1290-c.1340) and the Octagon at Ely (1322-53) are in the Decorated style, although when the latter was completed interest in the Decorated style was waning and making way for the Perpendicular style which continued until 1530, when it might more properly be called Tudor. Perpendicular is distinguished by the use of slender, vertically subdivided piers and large windows with cusped arches. The nave of Canterbury (c.1375) is an example of the style and the ultimate glory is Henry VII's chapel. Westminster Abbey (1503-12), only a few years later than King's College chapel, Cambridge (c.1475). It could with justification be claimed that the Tudor style of the sixteenth century was more Perpendicular than Renaissance.

Left. At Lincoln Cathedral (c.1200), the distinctive horizontal line below the Triforium distinguishes the Early English style (1200-1300).

Below. Windows in the Lady chapel (c.1320), Wells Cathedral, show geometrical tracery typical of the Decorated period.

CASTLES

The peak of castle-building came in the late thirteenth century under Edward I (1272-1307) and his castle architect, James of St George, from Savoy in France. The troublesome tribes in north Wales necessitated the building of ten royal castles, of which nine were on or near the coast and could be supplied conveniently and safely by sea. Work was undertaken on four 'lordship' castles at Chirk, Denbigh, Hawarden and Holt and on three captured Welsh-built castles at Cricceth, Dolwyddelan and Castell-y-Bere. Edward also licensed four barons to build or strengthen their castles in what is now Clwyd in return for grants of land. In all, some sixteen Edwardian castles were built in north Wales between 1272 and 1307 and, of these, four had concentric defences similar to the earlier Dover Castle plan.

Edward I's castle building was not confined to Wales. He carried out a major strengthening of the Tower of London and substantial work was carried out at St Briavels, Corfe, Leeds and Rockingham. Additionally, barons built or rebuilt their castles at Goodrich, Kidwelly, Carew, Carreg Cennon and Skipton. Edward I's abortive invasion of Scotland in 1296-7 resulted in his having to build new castles and rebuild or strengthen captured castles, a total of some seventeen, adding a high price to Edwardian aggression.

After the feverish building of the Edwardian reign, the following 200 years saw nothing like the same scale of castle building. Dunstanburgh, Northumberland, was built 1313-6, then scarcely any castles were built until Hadleigh, Essex, was begun in 1359 and Raby, Co. Durham (1381) and Tutbury, Staffordshire (1399-1460). Caister, Norfolk, was begun for Sir John Fastolf in 1432, the same year as the great tower at Tattershall, Lincolnshire, was built by Ralph, Lord Cromwell. Considerable work was done at Alnwick, Northumberland (1350), Bodiam (1385) and Hurstmonceux (1441), both in Sussex, Carlisle, County Durham (1378-83), Lancaster (1400) and Warwick (c.1450-94).

Bodiam Castle, East Sussex, begun 1385 and all of one period, rectangular with angle towers at the corners.

No sooner did castle builders devise new ways of defensive building than they were outwitted by besiegers. However, most castles built by the barons of England were for protection against outlaw bands. The testing bed was the Crusades to the Holy Land where castles withstood long sieges, doors were forced with battering rams and walls were undermined. In England, defence against this kind of assault, apart from the royal castles, was in the main unnecessary. Outlaws were not going to sit out a siege nor expensively construct tunnels to mine walls. The centre and strong point of medieval castles was the inner bailey, which might or might not enclose a keep. This was surrounded by one or more concentric walls with strategically placed towers, and a moat. The weak point was the entrance gate defended by flanking towers. Should attackers cross the drawbridge to attempt breaking down the door, a portcullis would fall cutting off their retreat. A rain of arrows fired on them from above through 'murder holes' effectively and efficiently ended the attack. However, the moat could be bridged, the portcullis jammed and a covered battering ram used to protect the attackers as they broke down the door.

Dover is perhaps the most impressive of medieval castles, the more so because it has been in continuous use to the present day. Begun *c.* 1170, the Constable's Gate, the last feature to be built, was not finished until 1227. Dover was besieged in 1216 and the eastern tower mined – it was only saved by the death of King John at Newark when the seige was called off.

Gunpowder and cannons were not entirely responsible for the decline of the castle. Quite simply, England became more peaceful by the fourteenth century and fortifications were no longer necessary to protect the powerful, except in the troublesome border area with Scotland. The common form of protection here was the pele-tower, of which there are over 200 in Northumberland alone but not all are medieval. The pele-tower (*see* p.25) was only effective against small-scale raids and of no use at all against a professional army. Livestock was herded into the undercroft and the family and servants took refuge in the upper storey until it was safe to come out again. Many Scottish castles retain the original pele-tower submerged by later, more substantial building, as at Hermitage, Borders Region, and Cawdor, Highland Region.

Although castles gradually became outmoded as a form of defence, they were still built as evidence of influence and authority. Ralph, Lord Cromwell, Lord Treasurer of England, was making such a statement when he rebuilt Tattershall in 1432-45. The great tower, 110 ft high, dominates the flat Lincolnshire landscape. Although surrounded by moats and walls, it could never have withstood an organised army nor was it intended to. The idea of castle-building as symbolic of power and authority continued long after such buildings had ceased to be militarily effective. One hundred years later, Henry VIII fearing invasion in the 1530s, built a succession of forts along the south coast, the largest being at Deal. These

The pele-tower shown here with projecting stair-turret, was an ideal defence against outlaw bands in the Border country with Scotland. Mainly medieval but some built in the fifteenth century.

Cawdor Castle, Highland Region. The original pele-tower in the centre was built c.1454 and now surrounded by later building.

Tattershall Castle, Lincolnshire. Built 1432-45 by Ralph Lord Cromwell as a statement of power. The tall brick keep dominates the flat countryside.

cannot properly be called castles as they were large, glorified gun platforms for firing at enemy shipping.

During the Civil War (1642-9) many castles were repaired and garrisoned and, although battered by cannons, held out against foes for many months and even years as at Newark, Nottinghamshire. To reduce their effectiveness, Lord Protector Cromwell ordered them to be 'slighted' and made undefendable. To him we owe the many castle ruins dotting our countryside.

Typical Features of Medieval Castles
Plan: The old conception of an inner keep was no longer possible because more accommodation was needed for larger numbers of defenders. Barracks were built within an inner bailey where great hall, chamber, kitchens and brewery were grouped. The angles of this wall were fortified by drum towers. The inner bailey would be surrounded by the outer bailey, which again would have drum towers giving fields of fire to cover the walls. The entrance gates were heavily defended with more towers. Beyond the outer wall as a moat and the entrances were defended by outlying 'barbicans'. The earliest barbican is at Dover.

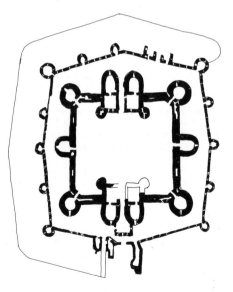

Plan of Beaumaris Castle, Gwynedd. A late addition to Edward I's strategic plan for North Wales, begun 1295, completed 1330, symmetrical with two concentric walls.

Elevation: Narrow openings either vertical or cruciform for cross-bow fire and later for guns, larger openings within the inner bailey. Wall thickness varies but never less than *c*.10ft and *c*.33-6ft in height.

SOME TYPES OF ARROW SLITS

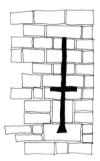

*Trematon
(Crosslet with
tailbottom)*

*Manorbier
(Top crosslet
with tailbottom)*

*Pembroke
(Slit with
rectangular oilet)*

Where to See Examples

North – *Alnwick* (D of Northumberland), Northumberland, 1309-50 restored in C18 and C19; *Aydon* (EH), Northumberland, hall and services C13, walls and defences 1315; *Bolton* (Hon. H. Orde-Powlett), North Yorkshire, begun 1375; *Dunstanburgh* (EH), Northumberland, C14; *Preston Tower* (Maj. Baker-Cresswell), Northumberland, pele-tower *c*.1400.

Midlands – *Ashby de la Zouche* (EH), Leicestershire, C15. Built by Lord Hastings; *Broughton* (Ld Saye & Sele), Oxfordshire, a fortified manor of the early C14, enlarged in 1550; *Goodrich* (EH), Hereford & Worcester, late C13 and C14; *Warwick* (Mme. Tussauds), Warwickshire, C14.

East – *Caister*, Norfolk, begun 1432, brick and unusual.

South – *Bodiam* (NT), East Sussex, 1385, fine example of moated courtyard castle; *Dartmouth* (EH), Devonshire, begun 1481; *Farnham* (EH), Surrey, C13 around a motte of *c*.1140; *Hever* (Broadlands Props. Ltd), Kent, moated fortified manor, 1340-80; *Leeds* (Leeds Castle Foundation), Kent, *c*.1278, restored C19; *Lympne* (Mr H. Margory), Kent, C14 restored 1905; *Nunney* (EH), Somerset, C14 in French style; *Powderham* (E of Devon), Devonshire, *c*.1390, restored and altered in C18 & C19; *Saltwood* (Hon. Alan Clark), Kent, *c*.1240; *Sudeley* (Ld Ashcombe), Gloucestershire, *c*.1440s.

Scotland – *Blair* (D of Atholl), Tayside Region, the Comyn Tower is of *c*.1270 engulfed in later additions; *Caerlaverock* (SSS), Dumfries & Galloway, triangular Edwardian *c*.1290-1300; *Castle Campbell* (SSS), Central Region, late-C14 tower with C15 and C16 additions;

Cawdor (E Cawdor), Grampian Region, tower 1454; *Dirleton* (SSS), Lothian Region, C13, C14 & C15; *Drum* (NTS), Grampian Region, late-C13 tower with later additions; *Dunvegan* (Mr J. MacLeod), Highlands Region, C13 tower with later additions; *Edinburgh* (HBM), Lothian Region, few buildings earlier than C17 remain; *Fyvie* (NTS), Grampian Region, SE tower *c*.1390-1430 with many later additions; *Hermitage* (SSS), Borders Region, massive tower-house *c*.1470; *Lennoxlove* (NTS), Lothian Region, L-plan tower *c*.1420 with later additions; *Neidpath* (Ly.E.Benson), L-plan tower house *c*.1490; *Stirling* (SSS), Central Region, C13, with fine renaissance Great Hall 1460-80.

Wales – *Beaumaris* (WHM), Gwynedd, splendid concentric plan 1292-1330; *Caernarvon* (WHM), Gwynedd, grandest Edwardian 1283-1320; *Caerphilly* (WHM), Glamorgan, largest in Wales and remarkable 1268-1327; *Carreg Cennon* (WHM), Dyfed, courtyard plan 1272-1307, ruined in Civil War; *Chepstow* (WHM), Gwent, great tower *c*.1070, barbican *c*.1245; *Chirk* (NT), Clwyd, 1282-1322; *Conwy* (WHM), Gwynedd, 1277-92; *Denbigh* (WHM), Clwyd, ruins of keep & curtain walls 1282; *Flint* (WHM), Clwyd, ruins of first of Edward I's castles 1277; *Harlech* (WHM), Gwynedd, concentric 1283-90; *Kidwelly* (WHM), Dyfed, concentric *c*.1275 and outer walls C14; *Raglan* (WHM), Gwent, hexagonal tower and two courtyards *c*.1435-1525; *Rudlan* (WHM), Clwyd, concentric Edwardian 1277-82.

CATHEDRALS AND CHURCHES

Medieval architecture reached its peak of eloquence just as it was to be superseded by the coming Renaissance. The technique of vaulting and of carrying immense pressures safely down slender, decorated piers was carried to the extreme and vast areas of glass brought streams of coloured light pouring down on altars and choirs. King's College chapel, Cambridge and Henry VII's chapel, Westminster Abbey, are supreme examples of this final brilliance never to be repeated.

This was architectural glory. There was also the glory of colour. However, that has gone from our churches, abbeys and cathedrals and a leap of imagination is needed to visualize them as they were. As conceived, the interiors and some exteriors of the buildings were ablaze with colour. The detail of the west front of Wells Cathedral was picked out in red, blue, green, black and ochre and the saints, possibly painted white, stood in niches of deep red. Small holes through the wall brought singing voices from the sculpted saints along the front from choirs hidden within – an early example of 'son et lumière'. The chapter house at Southwell Minster had the wildlife and leaves of the capitals picked out in natural colours, all scrubbed off in the late nineteenth century. Even small parish churches had instructive episodes from the scriptures painted on their walls with the inevitable 'Doom' painted over the crossing arch as an awful warning to all sinners, and some few survive. Doom paintings portrayed Christ in Majesty over the arch with the wicked to one side

Henry VII's chapel, Westminster, 1503-12, one of the supreme examples of late-Perpendicular style.

being pitchforked into the flames of Hell and the good rejoicing in Heaven with angels on the other.

As confidence in the new building techniques increased, so architects became more daring; windows became taller and wider, their openings filled with exuberant tracery. Windows, from the plate tracery in narrow pointed arches of *c*.1200 to wide four-centred arches of *c*.1500 filled with panel tracery, are a certain way of dating a building. The capitals of piers give other certain clues to dating from the stiff-leaf of Early English (1200-1300) through the nobbly of Decorated (1300-50) to the Perpendicular (1350-1530) when piers had become so slender that capitals had all but vanished.

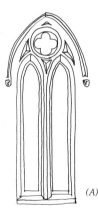

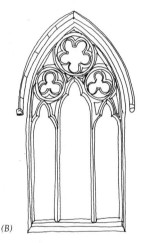

(A) Plate tracery C.13. (B) Geometrical (bar) tracery C.13. (C) Reticulated tracery C.13-14. (4) Late C.14 tracery.

Typical Features of the Early English Style 1200-1300

The style begins with Wells (*c.*1180) and Lincoln (1192) cathedrals in which there is a defined horizontal emphasis. The first star vaults are in the nave of Lincoln, reaching their peak of design in the mid fourteenth century at Exeter Cathedral. In the north, Rievaulx Abbey was built in the middle of this style and, although now a roof-less ruin, the church interior expresses to perfection the horizontal lines and even flow of simple pointed arches.

Above. Star-vaulting, Exeter Cathedral, 1327-69; the longest unbroken Gothic vault in the world and the peak of this skill.

Below. The ruined nave of Rievaulx Abbey, North Yorkshire, 1225-40: the strong horizontal lines are typical of the Early English style.

Plan: The early apsidal east bay was superseded by a square east end built further to the east. Aisles were added to naves and the plan becomes a series of rectangles.

Elevation: The pointed arch and horizontal line distinguish the exterior. Almost tentatively, windows become wider, placed in twos and threes between angled buttresses, as at Salisbury Cathedral. Like the straight-sided plan, the exterior consists of straight verticals and horizontals.

Roof: High pitched as at Salisbury Cathedral.

Windows: Plate tracery and bar tracery distinguish Early English; as masons become more confident in their abilities the tracery and mullions become lighter.

Decoration: Use of black Purbeck marble detached shafts as at Lincoln Cathedral. Capitals deeply carved in stiff-leaf fashion and all carvings, such as mouldings, are more undercut. Piscinas introduced near altars.

'Stiff-leaf' capital, typical of the late-twelfth and early thirteenth centuries.

Typical Features of the Decorated Style 1300-1350

Plan: In place of the straight-sided plan, angles were introduced giving interesting windows and oblique plays of light. The polygonal chapter house at Southwell is a good example.

Elevation: Buttressed walls mark out bays in 12-15ft widths, the buttresses rising to pinnacles above the parapet in set-off steps. The parapet, becoming battlemented by 1340, conceals guttering from which rain water flows through projecting gargoyle spouts.

Windows: Lancet windows with heavy plate tracery and pointed arches give way to lighter and freer tracery in geometrical shapes, trefoils, multifoils. Intersecting and reticulated traceries in the window head mark the latter years of this period. Lincoln Cathedral is a supreme example.

Roof: Low-pitched and lead-covered timber, supported by hammerbeams, decorative work, originally painted. Good examples of this in Suffolk. Complex stone vaulting in the aisles.

Tower: The great west door was used for processions, consequently the west front increased in importance. Towers, supported by angled buttresses, became common at the west end of churches.

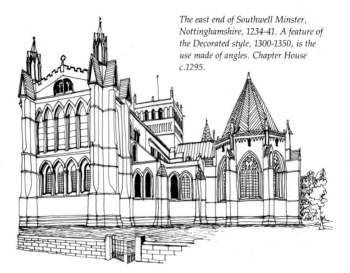

The east end of Southwell Minster, Nottinghamshire, 1234-41. A feature of the Decorated style, 1300-1350, is the use made of angles. Chapter House c.1295.

Intersecting and reticulated traceried window. Decorated period 1300-50.

Typical Features of the Perpendicular Style 1350-1530

The final flowering of the Gothic style, when stonework became so light as to resemble lace and vaulting achieved extraordinary lightness with ribs, liernes and tiercerons weaving geometrical shapes. The style is characterized by slender, vertically subdivided supports and little fantasy in the window tracery. The hallmark is the panel motif of cusped arches. This appears everywhere in rows, in traceries and on walls. The grandest churches are in the wool counties of Norfolk, Suffolk, the Cotswolds and in Somerset.

STAR VAULTING

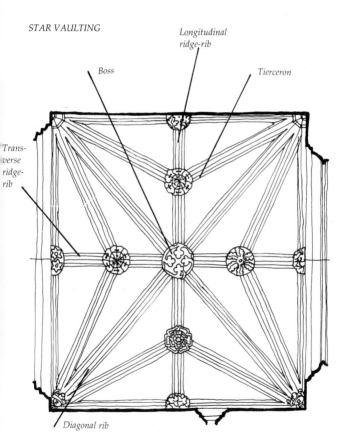

Longitudinal ridge-rib

Boss

Tierceron

Transverse ridge-rib

Diagonal rib

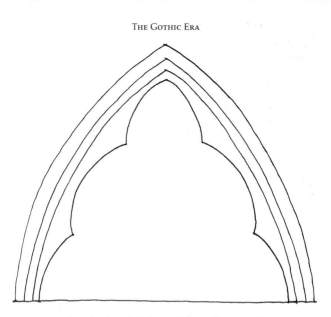

Cusped arch, typical of the early Perpendicular period.

Window in late-Perpendicular style of c.1450 with a four-centre arch and square hood-mould to deflect rain water.

Elevation: Large, wide windows placed between buttresses rising to crocketed finials, clerestory windows in nave, lighter flying buttresses, battlemented parapets, tall towers, with string-courses marked with panels of diaper work. Walls finished in fine ashlar.
Windows: Tracery consisting chiefly of vertical members the tops filled with geometrical designs, in a four-centred arch, squared hood moulds. Panel tracery is the typical Perpendicular feature.

Where to See Examples of Cathedrals
North – *Carlisle*, Cumbria, tower, north arm of transept and stalls C15; *Durham*, County Durham, eastern transept C15; *Ripon*, North Yorkshire, west front C13, central tower C15; *York*, North Yorkshire, north and south transepts 1225-55, chapter-house 1260-90, nave and west front 1291-*c*.1345, east end 1361-1402, central tower completed 1470s, south-west tower 1432-56.
Midlands – *Chester*, Cheshire, chapter-house 1250, choir C14, crossing C14; *Hereford*, Herefordshire & Worcester, north transept C13,

Diaper-work decoration popular in the Perpendicular period from 1350 onwards.

central tower C16; **Lincoln**, Lincolnshire, transept and choir 1207-20, repairs to west front 1218, chapter-house 1220-5 and 1307, nave 1227-40, central tower c.1240, Angel Choir 1256-80, Bishop's eye window c.1375; **Lichfield**, Staffordshire, transept and chapter-house C13, nave late C13, central tower, Lady chapel and presbytery C14; **Southwell**, Nottinghamshire, east transept C13, chapter-house late C13; **Worcester**, Worcestershire, choir C13, nave C14, central tower 1357-74.

East – **Ely**, Cambridgeshire, choir C13, Lady chapel, choir, octagon and lantern C14; **Norwich**, Norfolk, west front and nave vault C15; **Peterborough**, Cambridgeshire, central tower C14, extension of east end C15-C16.

South – **Bath**, Avon, presbytery, transept, nave and west front 1496-1539; **Canterbury**, Kent, part of chapter-house C14, south-west tower C15; **Exeter**, Devon, chapter-house C13, presbytery, choir, crossing and nave C13-C14, west front C14; **Gloucester**, Gloucestershire, nave vault C13, south aisle 1318-26, cloisters 1375-1410, central tower C15; **Oxford**, Oxfordshire, Lady chapel, Latin chapel C14; **Rochester**, Kent, choir 1220-7, north transept c.1240, south transept c.1280, completion of central tower 1343; **St Albans**, Hertfordshire, west front late C12-C13, presbytery C13, Lady chapel C14; **Salisbury**, Wiltshire, church 1220-58, west front 1266, chapter-house 1265-75, upper tower C14; **Wells**, Somerset, transept and nave late C12-C13, west front C13, chapter-house late-C13, Lady chapel and central tower C14; **Westminster**, Lady chapel 1220, presbytery, ambulatory, transept and chapter-house 1246-59, west window and nave roof 1471-98, completion of nave vault 1498-1502, Henry VII's Chapel 1512; **Winchester**, Hampshire, Lady chapel and retro-choir c.1202, presbytery C14, west front late C14, remodelling of nave late C14-C15.

Scotland – **Elgin**, Grampian Region, begun 1224, now ruined; **Glasgow**, Strathclyde, all C13.

Wales – **Brecon**, Powys, chancel, transept and tower C13, chapels in north and south transepts C14; **Llandaff**, Glamorgan, church C12-C13, Lady chapel C13, chapter-house c.1250; **St David's**, Dyfed, presbytery 1215-?, collapse of central tower 1220, and repairs c.1275-?, Lady chapel chapter-house 1328-47.

MONASTERIES

A monastery is a residence for monks dedicated to the religious life. An abbey is governed by an abbot and a priory by a prior. Some establishments also had nuns beneath their roof but more commonly nuns inhabited convents. When, in its early stages in the Middle East, monasticism was practised in the eremetical (hermit) form, monasteries were merely groups of huts or cells. As time went on the monks erected massive buildings surrounded by high walls and monastic life became communal. As we have already seen, monasticism came to Britain in the sixth century, from Ireland in the north of England and from Rome in the south.

The policy of the early English kings was to give land to the Church knowing that the clergy would maintain law and order on their estates. Consequently the medieval Church was wealthy and becoming wealthier. Monasteries were established and became sanctuaries of security in troubled times, and centres of learning and healing. The first gardens were made within monasteries' walls, established to grow medicinal herbs and flowers for religious processions. In this world, there were no national frontiers, ideas flowed back and forth across the Channel regardless of the hazards and difficulty of travelling huge distances. The monastic revival by St Benedict (480-543) was the cause of the greatest number of fine

(1) Church. (2) Chapter-house. (3) Frater. (4) Kitchen. (5) Lay-brothers' Dorter above. (6) Lay-brothers' Rere-dorter. (7) Brothers' Dorter above. (8) Brothers' Rere-dorter. (9) Warming House. (10) Infirmary. (11) Abbot's chamber.

monasteries. At the Reformation there were nearly 300 Benedictine monasteries and nunneries in England; they were by far the largest order. In Scotland, the Cistercians were the most numerous order, having eleven monasteries. The Augustinian, the Premonstratensian, the Cistercian and the small Cluniac orders had sprung from the Benedictines and had different rules, but the layout of their buildings was similar to those of the Benedictines. The plan of these establishments was standard as far as the site allowed. The church was the centre of the monastic life and cloisters were attached to the south wall of its south aisle. Augustinian churches are distinguished by their enormous length.

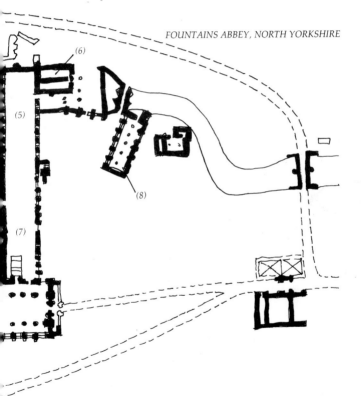

FOUNTAINS ABBEY, NORTH YORKSHIRE

Fountains, a Cistercian abbey in Yorkshire, is typical of the layout. On the east side of the cloister was the chapter house, the 'committee room' of the establishment, with the monks' dormitory, or 'dorter', lying to its south. Close to the river Skell, to the back of the dorter, were the latrines, or 'rere-dorter'. Along the south side of the cloister were the dining hall, or 'frater', the kitchen and the warming house, the only heated space apart from the kitchen. The west side of the cloister was taken up with the lay-brothers' dorter over a cellar. Other buildings to the east comprised a large infirmary with its own kitchen, a prison and the abbot's lodgings. Fountains was a large complex designed to accommodate more than fifty monks and over 200 lay-brothers. Cistercians were forbidden unnecessary decoration and sites were usually wild, desolate. Their chapter houses were always quadrangular and separated into two or three aisles by piers and arches.

The exception to the standard monastic plan was that adopted by the small Carthusian order. The order sprang up when eremetical monasticism was revived by St Bruno (1050-1102) and solitude and silence were enforced. There were no dorters or fraters for communal living and, instead, each monk had his own cottage and garden placed around a square cloister and cemetery. Their church was beyond this 'great cloister'. The typical Carthusian plan is best seen at Mount Grace in Yorkshire.

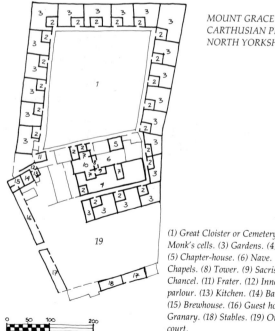

MOUNT GRACE
CARTHUSIAN PRIORY,
NORTH YORKSHIRE

(1) Great Cloister or Cemetery. (2) Monk's cells. (3) Gardens. (4) Garden. (5) Chapter-house. (6) Nave. (7) Chapels. (8) Tower. (9) Sacristy. (10) Chancel. (11) Frater. (12) Inner parlour. (13) Kitchen. (14) Bakehouse. (15) Brewhouse. (16) Guest house. (17) Granary. (18) Stables. (19) Outer court.

The peak of monastic expansion was in the late twelfth and early thirteenth centuries. Due to the great wealth generated from agriculture and the rents of large ecclesiastical estates, there was little need to economize in building. The Black Death of 1348-9 seriously reduced the number of monks and lay-brothers and by 1500 there were as few as 10,000 monks and 2,000 nuns in England. It all came to a sudden end. The final blow in England was the Dissolution under Henry VIII in 1536-40. In Scotland the Reformation was equally destructive; there is hardly a roofed medieval cathedral or monastery left.

Rievaulx Abbey, to take one example, sited in a well-watered and sloping valley in Yorkshire, was founded in 1131. Within ten years there were 300 Cistercian monks and lay-brothers and by 1150, 140 monks supported by 600 lay-brothers. This rapid expansion inevitably caused rebuilding, leaving the abbey seriously in debt – the church was completed in the mid-twelfth century and extended in the thirteenth. The Black Death cut back the monastic establishment and by 1380 Rievaulx was reduced to only fifteen monks and three lay-brothers. Parts of the chapter house, warming house and dorter

Rievaulx Abbey, North Yorkshire, a typical Cistercian plan.

were removed in the late fifteenth century because they were too big for the few occupants. When the abbey was dissolved in 1538, the lead from the roofs, the glass, woodwork and furniture were sold and the stone became a useful quarry for local builders. So the once great abbey became the romantic ruin it is today. The story can be repeated many times in the histories of other great monastic establishments. However, there is one difference at Rievaulx: due to the steep slope of the valley the church is sited north and south instead of the customary east to west, although contemporary writers always refer to the chancel being 'at the east end'.

Where to See Examples

North – **Brinkburn** (EH), Northumberland, Augustinian, founded 1135; **Fountains** (EH), North Yorkshire, Cistercian, founded 1132; **Furness** (EH), Lancashire, Cistercian, founded 1123; **Guisborough** (EH), Cleveland, Augustinian, founded 1119; **Lindisfarne** (EH), Northumberland, Benedictine, founded 1083; **Monk Bretton** (EH), Cluniac, founded 1154; **Mount Grace** (EH), North Yorkshire, Carthusian, founded 1398; **Rievaulx** (EH), North Yorkshire, Cistercian, founded 1131; **Roche** (EH), South Yorkshire, Cistercian, founded 1147; **Whitby** (EH), North Yorkshire, Benedictine, refounded 1078.

Midlands – **Buildwas** (EH), Shropshire, Cistercian, founded 1135; **Crowland**, Lincolnshire, Benedictine, founded 971; **Hailes** (EH), Gloucestershire, Cistercian, founded 1246; **Haughmond** (EH), Shropshire, Augustinian, founded 1130s; **Much Wenlock**, Shropshire, Cluniac, refounded 1050.

East – **Castle Acre** (EH), Norfolk, Cluniac, founded 1089; **Walsingham** (Walsingham Ests.), Norfolk, Augustinian, founded 1169; **Bury St Edmunds** (EH), Suffolk, Benedictine, founded 1020; **Thetford** (EH), Norfolk, Cluniac, founded 1103.

South – **Battle** (EH), East Sussex, Benedictine, founded 1067; **Cleeve** (EH), Somerset, Cistercian, founded 1198; **Glastonbury** (EH), Benedictine, refounded 705; **Netley** (EH), Hampshire, Cistercian, founded 1239.

Scotland – **Coldringham** (SSS) Borders Region, Benedictine, founded 1139; **Crossragruel** (SSS), Strathclyde, Cluniac, early C13; **Dryburgh** (SSS), Borders Region, Premonstratensian, founded 1150; **Dundrennan** (SSS), Dumfries & Galloway, Cistercian, founded 1140; **Jedburgh** (SSS), Borders Region, Augustinian, founded 1138; **Kelso** (SSS), Borders Region, Benedictine, founded 1113; **Melrose** (SSS), Borders Region, Cistercian, founded c. 1140; **Sweetheart** (SSS), Borders Region, Cistercian, founded 1273.

Wales – **Bassingwerk** (WHM), Clwyd, Cistercian, founded 1131; **Cymer** (WHM), Gwynedd, Cistercian, founded 1198-9; **Ewenny** (WHM), Mid-Glamorgan, Benedictine, founded 1141; **Llantony** (WHM), Gwent, Augustinian, founded 1108; **St Dogmael's** (WHM), Dyfed, Tironensian, founded 1113-5; **Strata Florida** (WHM), Cistercian, founded 1164; **Talley** (WHM), Dyfed, Premonstratensian, founded 1189; **Tintern** (WHM), Gwent, Cistercian, founded 1131; **Valle Crucis** (WHM), Clwyd, Cistercian, founded 1201.

HOUSES

The 'open hall' plan compared with the larger domestic and fortified buildings has already been discussed. A similar hall plan applied to the humblest dwelling varying only in the number or lack of rooms off the hall. Surviving inventories of even the smallest cottage of only one room have referred to 'goods in the hall' and then listed the few pathetic artefacts of the deceased. Hall is a French term; in parts of Britain it was called the 'house', or the 'house place', derived from Norse but meaning the same thing. The rule is that all medieval houses of any size had a hall. With this in mind, we can more easily understand the layout of medieval dwellings.

Off the upper end of the hall of a more substantial dwelling of the better-off would be a parlour serving as the main bedchamber. Over this would be an upper chamber used for storage and serving as a secondary bedchamber for other members of the family. This is often mistakenly called the 'solar', but the term means any upper chamber, even if it is in the roof-space. To the other end, on the longer sides of the hall, were two entrance doors facing each other. This arrangement caused frightful draughts and a screen was placed across the width so making what is called the 'screens passage'. Off the screen were two rooms for storage, the pantry for dry-goods such as flour and bread, and the buttery for wet-goods like milk, butter and cheese. Cooking was done in the hall over a central hearth. This type of building with jettied, or outward projecting, first floor to the upper chambers is found all over the Weald of Kent and is known as the 'Wealden house'. In fact, it is not confined to the Weald but is found all over the south-east and East Anglia. Dating from the late fourteenth to fifteenth centuries the Wealden house was the mark of a prosperous yeoman.

At the Weald and Downland Open Air Museum, near Chichester, a Wealden house of exactly this type is re-erected in its original late medieval state and without glass in the hall window. It was once the home of a well-to-do yeoman farmer, but to live in it today would be impossible. Smoke hangs heavily about making one's eyes run and draughts penetrate the ill-fitting window shutters and blow through the cracks between the timbers and round the screen. Even in this type of well-to-do dwelling there was little scope for architectural frills; the window heads might have cusped arches and the main doors four-centre arches. Otherwise, all is finished in straight sides. It was in the roof timbers, exposed over the hall, that the medieval carpenter could exhibit his skill.

Little in the way of architecture is found in the better built manor houses of stone. Doors and window heads gave scope for traceries, and fireplaces on side walls sometimes have decorated canopies. Like the smaller yeoman houses, the roof timbers of the hall can be highly decorative constructions.

In the grander houses cooking was done in a kitchen, often separate. The screens passage would have had three doors of service with the centre one leading to the kitchen. Haddon Hall, Derbyshire, shows these developments well. The great hall, wrongly called the 'Banqueting Hall', was built *c*.1370 with a parlour to one end and the services behind the screens passage at the other. In the mid fifteenth century the hearth was moved to a side wall and a new screen installed. By the mid sixteenth century this layout had become out-dated and the family, requiring more privacy, made a great chamber by ceiling over the parlour and moving upstairs. But privacy as such would have meant little to the medieval mind. The wealthy lived among their household and servants were everywhere. Lower down the social scale, the yeoman farmer lived with his farm ser-vants. In the first half of the sixteenth century the pattern of the family retreating into their great chamber was being followed in many manor houses. The yeoman class followed the fashion in the late sixteenth and early seventeenth centuries by ceiling over their halls to provide more upper floor accommodation.

Although the medieval and even Tudor floor plan was almost uni-versal, the materials of which houses were built varied according to what was locally available. A belt of good building limestone runs

Part section of a Wealdon house of c.1450. The upper room on the left is the Chamber, beneath on the ground-floor is the Parlour, to the right is the Hall open to the rafters.

Working in timber did not allow the scope for decoration as in stone. An exception is in the roof timbers of the Hall where the carpenter shows his skill.

Haddon Hall, Derbyshire. The Great Hall built 1350. The central hearth was moved to the left-hand wall in c.1450 and the screen renewed. Re-roofed 1930s.

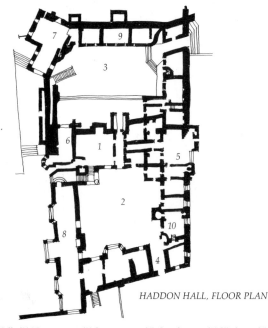

HADDON HALL, FLOOR PLAN

(1) Great Hall. (2) Upper court. (3) Lower court. (4) Gate-houses. (5) Kitchens. (6) Parlour. (7) Chapel. (8) Gallery. (9) Lodgings. (10) Bakery.

from the Mendips in the south to the uplands of south Yorkshire. Sandstone in Sussex, south Wales and Cumbria was almost as good, although it weathers badly if not laid on its bed or is not of the best quality. The hard granite of parts of Devon and Cornwall and of north Wales and the Lakes provided its own particular building character in which decoration was almost impossible due to the un-relenting nature of the material. Elsewhere, flint was used in the eastern counties and even mud or clay mixed with straw, called cob, in parts of Devon, Cornwall on on the Cambridgeshire borders with Norfolk and Suffolk. Despite its unpromising nature, cob proved durable and cottages made of it survive to this day.

It is in the areas where timber was available that half-timbered buildings survive in their hundreds. The term applies to those build-ings constructed of a series of timber sections strengthened by braces, the spaces filled in with plaster or brickwork, called 'nog-ging'. The unfortunate nineteenth-century fashion of staining timber black has deprived us of the silver-grey colour of old oak that once gave the street scene a more mellow appearance. In other once forested areas, such as Sherwood Forest in Nottinghamshire, there were also many half-timbered buildings; but the local clay makes excellent bricks and, as the timber buildings fell into disrepair, they were replaced in brick in the late eighteenth and early nineteenth centuries.

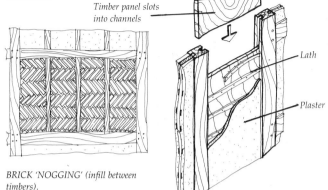

Timber panel slots into channels

Lath

Plaster

BRICK 'NOGGING' (infill between timbers).

PLASTER INFILL

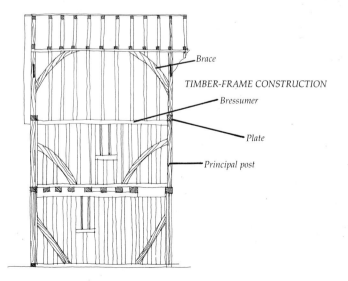

Brace

TIMBER-FRAME CONSTRUCTION

Bressumer

Plate

Principal post

There are regional variations also in the construction of half-timbered buildings. The 'cruck-truss', forming the walls and roof in one frame and once thought to be entirely medieval, continued to be utilized into the nineteenth century. Available only to smaller buildings owing to the size of tree needed, crucks are found in west, central and northern England and most of Wales. The timber-framed construction consisted of a number of vertical frames held by horizontal timbers called 'plates'. Both cruck and timber-framed buildings are similar in construction; the timber-framed type was used for even the largest buildings. In the eastern parts of the country the timber 'box-frame' was universal. This consisted of building the house as a box, the roof being a separate construction. This practice was perhaps originally designed for stone-built houses and later applied to timber construction. In areas where the two methods of building meet, as in the Midlands, the two styles are mixed and even a hybrid form was often used. The key to recognizing a cruck, or the derivative timber-framed building, is through the roof purlins which project through the gable-end and are often joined by a heavy collar-beam whereas the roof of the box-framed building lacks purlins and the gable-end is plain. Throughout the medieval period the principal roofing material was straw or reed thatch. In stone areas, such as Gloucestershire, stone tiles were used for roofing and, in the clay lands, clay tiles were used from the 1300s.

Cruck construction. The end of the cottage shows the 'Cruck-truss' made out of two curved timbers. Note the absence of roof purlins.

BOX-FRAME CONSTRUCTION

(A) The frame made with posts held by braces. (B) Corner detail on brick or stone plinth. (C) Sequence of building. (D) Roof is separate construction.

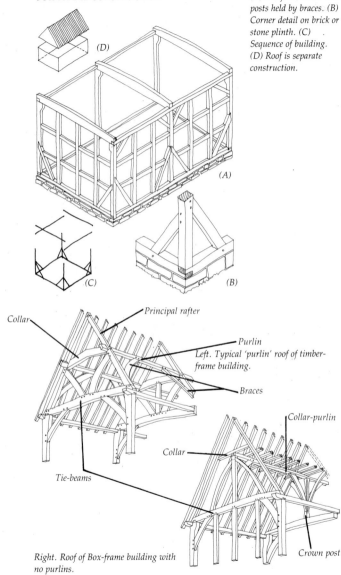

(D)

(A)

(C)

(B)

Collar

Principal rafter

Purlin

Left. Typical 'purlin' roof of timber-frame building.

Braces

Collar-purlin

Collar

Tie-beams

Crown post

Right. Roof of Box-frame building with no purlins.

In Scotland abundant stone provided building material and the pele-tower was the standard for many centuries until the Union with England in 1707 brought an overdue respite from border wars and skirmishes. In the Border area the pele-tower was known as a 'stone-house', indicating that other dwellings, now long vanished, were of timber. It has already been shown that the plan of the pele-tower was the vertical version of the hall-house. The Scottish pele-tower was expanded with additions, eventually developing into the Scottish Baronial style, which was based more on French influence than on English. Most Scots, however, lived in primitive style in stone, peat, or turf huts shared with their animals. This was no different from the medieval farming population of the uplands and poor soil areas in the rest of Britain which lived in various sizes of longhouse, sharing their roofs with their livestock. The history of this building extends over many centuries; in the north from the ninth century and in the south from the twelfth century. Some longhouses survive in Devon and Cornwall.

A seventeenth century Devonshire 'long house' in which the roof is shared on the right with farm animals in the 'byre'. The plan is universal throughout Britain in the north from the ninth century to the twelfth in the south.

Typical Features of the Smaller Medieval House

Plan: Four main types: Pele-tower, and three variations of the hall plan: (1) Double-ended hall with two wings. (2) Single-ended hall with one wing. (3) Hall house built with no wings. Early halls often had aisles; the roof-span was extended by means of upright posts to give extra width to the hall. Northern longhouses had one-and-a-half storeys and were larger than those in the south, which were usually of one storey with perhaps loft space.

Elevation: Local building materials used, ranging from stone to cob and half-timbering, with brick in the eastern counties from the four-teenth century. Many buildings of mixed materials, particularly the half-timbered type, where the infill of the panels, originally wattle and daub, was replaced in brick. Chimneys of stone and brick to

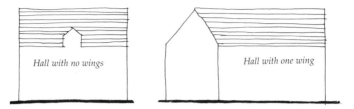

Hall with no wings

Hall with one wing

SIXTEENTH-CENTURY HOUSE-TYPES

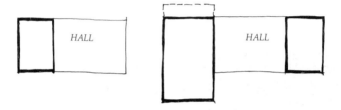

HALL

HALL

HALL

Hall with two wings

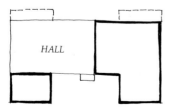

HALL

reduce the fire-hazard are common. In the half-timbered construction there are huge variations in the patterns used in the panels and on bargeboards, particularly in Cheshire and Lancashire. Outward projecting, or 'jettied', upper floors in half-timbered buildings are an early medieval practice; they became very common in the late fifteenth century.

Roof: Originally, most were thatched in straw or reed. Many were re-roofed in more durable materials; a tell-tale for this is a projecting ledge left on chimneys and walls. Other materials were clay tiles from the fourteenth century, stone slates in stone country and slate in Wales. Many slates were transported by canal from Wales in the late eighteenth and nineteenth centuries.

Detail of a half-timbered house showing a jetted first floor.

Windows and Doors: In early buildings windows were unglazed and protected by wooden shutters. Glass was expensive until the mid sixteenth century when it was set in small diamond-shaped leaded lights. Casement windows were introduced with glass and mullions and transomes of wood (or stone in stone counties). Where a hall was 'ceiled over' the tall windows are made into two smaller windows. Detailing around doors is found mainly in buildings of stone; pointed arches from the fourteenth to fifteenth centuries. The Tudor four-centred arch dates from the late fifteenth century.

Where to See Examples (Stone-built unless otherwise stated)
North – **Markenfield Hall** (Ld Grantley) Ripon, North Yorkshire, L-plan with 1st floor hall, early C14; **Rufford Old Hall** (NT), nr Ormskirk, Lancs, late-C15 to early-C16 timber-framed great hall with brick-built wing of *c.*1662; **Samlesbury** (Samlesbury Hall Trust), nr Preston, Lancs, C14 & *c.*1545 timber-framed manor; **Shandy Hall** (L. Sterne Trust), Coxwold, North Yorkshire, small C15 hall house in stone; **Shibden Hall** (Calderdale MBC), Halifax, West Yorkshire, C15 timber-framed hall house with later additions; **Turton Tower** (Lancs CC), Blackburn, Lancs, rare example of an English tower-house C15, with later additions.
Midlands – **Adlington Hall** (Mr C. Leigh), Macclesfield, Cheshire, hall *c.*1500, with additions of C17 & C18; **Avoncroft Museum of Buildings**, Stoke Heath, Bromsgrove, open-air architectural museum includes a C15 timber-framed house; **Baddesley Clinton** (NT), Solihull, Warwickshire, moated manor dating from C14; **Chester**, Cheshire, many examples of timber-framed town houses, over-restored in late C19; **Coughton Court** (NT), Alcester, Warwickshire, impressive gate-house 1509 with two wings added in late C16 with half-timbered upper stories; **Donnington-le-Heath Manor** (Leics Mus. Service), nr Coalville, Leicestershire, first-floor hall over undercroft *c.*1280; **Gainsborough Old Hall** (EH), Gainsborough, Lincolnshire, C15 timber-framed great hall, east and west wings timber-framed and brick *c.*1600; **Gawsworth Hall** (Mr & Mrs T. Richards), Macclesfield, Cheshire, L-plan timber-framed C16; **The Grey Friars** (NT), Worcester, Hereford & Worcester, timber-framed town house 1480, with later additions; **Haddon Hall** (D of Rutland), nr Bakewell, Derbyshire, hall, parlour and services of *c.*1370, restored in early C20; **Hall i'th' Wood** (Bolton MB), Bolton, Greater Manchester, timber-framed *c.*1500 with wing of *c.*1600; **Holme Pierrepont Hall** (Mr & Mrs R. Brackenbury) nr Nottingham, Nottinghamshire, remnant of large courtyard house, brick-built lodgings early C16; **Little Moreton Hall** (NT), Congleton, Cheshire, timber-framed throughout, hall *c.*1480, additions *c.*1559 and gallery *c.*1570; **Longthorpe Tower** (EH), nr Peterborough, Cambridgeshire, rare tower-house for England, C14, with contemporary wall paintings; **Lower Brockhampton** (NT), Bringsty, Hereford & Worcester, half-timbered manor house *c.*1400; **Norbury Hall** (NT), Ashbourne, Derbyshire, first-floor hall over undercroft *c.*1250; **Stratford-upon-**

Avon, many timber-framed town houses of C15 & C16.

East – *Nether Hall* (Mr B.T. Ambrose), Cavendish, Suffolk, timber-framed farmhouse of *c*.1500; *Otley Hall* (Mr J.G. Mosesson), nr Ipswich, Suffolk, half-timbered open hall and parlour *c*.1485; *Paycocke's* (NT), Coggeshall, Essex, merchant's house *c*.1500.

South – *Carew Manor* (London B of Sutton), Sutton, London, late-medieval hall with hammer-beam roof; *Dodington Hall* (Lady Gass), nr Bridgwater, Somerset, small Tudor manor house *c*.1500; *Filching Manor* (Mr P. Foulkes-Halbard), nr Polegate, East Sussex, open-hall, buttery and upper chamber, Wealden type *c*.1450; *Great Chalfield Manor* (NT), nr Melksham, Wiltshire, open-hall, great chamber and timber-framed wing all of 1467-88; *St Mary's House* (Mr P. Thorogood), Bramber, West Sussex, the best late-C15 timber-framing in Sussex; *Stoneacre* (NT), Otham, Kent, hall with open-timber roof *c*.1500, much restored in 1920; *Weald & Downland Museum*, Singleton, nr Chichester, West Sussex, open-air architectural museum including many timber-framed buildings; *Westminster Hall*, Palace of Westminster, London SW1, spectacular hammer-beam roof 1394-1402; *Whitehall* (London B of Sutton), Cheam, Surrey, timber-framed, weatherboarded farmhouse *c*.1500; *Little Sodbury Manor* (Mr & Mrs G. Harford), Chipping Sodbury, Avon, fine C15 hall with open timber roof.

South-West – *Athelhampton* (Ly Cooke), nr Dorchester, Dorset, hall with open timber roof *c*.1493, Tudor additions; *Bradley Manor* (NT), nr Newton Abbot, Devon, unspoilt manor house of C15; *Bull House* (Mr M.L. Corney), Pilton, Barnstable, Devon, late medieval great hall with open timbered roof; *King John's Hunting Lodge* (NT), Axbridge, Somerset, timber-framed merchant's house of *c*.1500; *Kirkham House* (EH), Paignton, Devon, merchant's house C15; *Purse Caundle Manor* (Mr M. de Pelet), nr Sherborne, Dorset, hall of *c*.1470 with Tudor additions.

Scotland – *Claypotts Castle* (SSS), Tayside Region, C16 tower-house with additions; *Crathes Castle* (NTS), Grampian Region, C16 tower-house with additions; *Provost Skene's House* (Aberdeen DC), Aberdeen, Grampian Region, L-plan of *c*.1545, the oldest house in Aberdeen; *The Town House* (NTS), Culross, Fife Region, example of C17 Scottish burgh architecture.

Wales – *Aberconwy House* (NT), Conwy, Gwynedd, town house C14; *Cochwillan Old Hall* (Mr R.C.H. Douglas Pennant), Talybont, Bangor, Gwynedd, hall of *c*.1400; *Tudor Merchant's House* (NT), Tenby, Dyfed, merchant's house, late-C15; *Ty Mawr Wybrnant* (NT), nr Penmachno, Gwynedd, large cottage, and birthplace of Bishop William Morgan in *c*.1545.

The Classical Era

Tudor and Jacobean 1530-1620

Renaissance is an Italian word meaning 'rebirth'. Today, the term means Italian art and architecture from *c*.1440 to the mid sixteenth century, but this was not always the case. In the sixteenth century travellers saw the Roman remains throughout southern Europe as evidence of a past civilization far superior to their own. Roman manuscripts survived in monastic libraries including the treatise *De Architectura* written *c*.46 B.C. by Vitruvius. These gave further evidence of a past, great civilization. The Renaissance was a conscious attempt to restore ancient Roman standards and motifs and in some cases to restore even a Roman way of living. Henry VII claimed a spurious descent from Brutus the Trojan to give his Welsh ancestry credibility. Although the Renaissance originated in Italy in the fourteenth century and gradually spread over western Europe, it was late in coming to England owing to Tudor policy – even if (as there is some evidence) Henry VIII attempted to introduce French Renaissance Court procedure.

At Henry VIII's death in 1547 England was isolated from the mainstream of Renaissance culture in Italy both ecclesiastically, and therefore intellectually, as well as geographically. Travelling to Roman Catholic countries was strongly discouraged. Only the Netherlands was accessible and both patrons and architects seized on the pattern books coming from the Low Countries as a source of the new style. The result is that English architecture is not a true Renaissance style but a mixture of misunderstood decorative details applied to buildings constructed to a medieval plan. Decorative details of Flemish strapwork and misunderstood classical motifs culled from pattern books were applied like a cosmetic to buildings of the same medieval hall plan as was discussed in the last section.

The cause of this backwardness is to be found in Court practice. Henry VIII maintained a large and costly medieval court, a practice his successors saw no reason to alter. Court life was centred on the Presence Chamber, the Great Hall, where lesser courtiers had always eaten, and on the Privy Chamber where the King ate. Higher ranking courtiers ate their meals, after the King had finished, in what in other households was called the Great Chamber.

For any courtier building a 'courtier-house', it was essential to provide accommodation against a time when they might entertain their monarch. Such a house of consequence built in the sixteenth century had a great hall and a range of state apartments consisting of great chamber, withdrawing chamber and bedchamber for a visiting monarch. Additionally, there were less grand family apartments with the same sequence of rooms. Such a sequence of family rooms is found in most gentry houses, and was used to accommodate high-ranking visitors when the family moved into other rooms. Unfortunately, Renaissance symmetry ran against this layout.

Details of architectural decorations used 1580-1620. 'This interwoven 'strapwork' design came from the Netherlands and was derived from decorative book plates of leather straps'.

This arrangement of rooms in grand houses had ceased in France in the early sixteenth century. French palaces had a floor-plan consisting of a large central room off which were apartments of three or four rooms, and this layout was reflected in the external symmetry. Until English Court practice changed on the accession of James I in 1603 nothing could be done.

There were some who aspired to being patrons of the Renaissance. Longleat in Wiltshire, a small medieval priory, was bought by Sir John Thynne in 1540. Enlarged, burnt down in 1567 and rebuilt on a grand scale, Longleat remains the earliest surviving example of English Renaissance architecture. Nevertheless, the interior layout was still the medieval floor-plan of hall, great chamber, withdrawing chamber and state bedchamber. All that remains of this interior is the hall. The exterior, which is Renaissance, is due to a Frenchman Alan Maynard, a mason who worked at Longleat from 1570. With him was an English mason, Robert Smythson, who came to Longleat in 1567 and went on to build and work as architect for many other courtier-houses mainly in the Midlands. Although a mason, he was the first in England to be called an architect.

Longleat House, Wiltshire: The earliest surviving true Renaissance house in England, built around a Carthusian monastery for Sir John Thynne from 1547 to 1580 by a French architect, Alan Maynard, and Robert Smythson.

Wollaton Hall, Nottingham, a surprising and extraordinary building of 1580-88 by Robert Smythson for a difficult patron, Sir Francis Willoughby. The classical details were taken from architectural pattern-books.

Wollaton Hall near Nottingham, built in 1580-8 by Smythson for a very difficult patron, Sir Francis Willoughby, is another expression of the English Renaissance. Unlike Longleat no one involved in its building had any direct experience of French architecture, though Willoughby had a very good library of architectural books that he used as a source to embellish his house. Like Longleat, the interior layout was the usual succession of hall, great chamber, etc. However, there were some startling differences. To overcome the problem faced by all builders who put a symmetrical façade on a hall, a space entered from one end, Smythson, or Willoughby, put the hall, lit by clerestory windows, in the very centre of the building and it was entered by a circuitous route. The state apartments on the first floor mark the biggest departure, although it is doubtful if Willoughby realized how radical he was being. He provided his new house with two sets of state apartments, one for a king and the other for a queen. This was some thirty years before its time in England but in line with French practice. Unfortunately, all this splendour, except the hall, was swept away by the architect Wyatville in the early nineteenth century. The first royal visit to Wollaton was in June 1603 when Queen Anne and Prince Henry used the two suites of rooms. Both were familiar with French custom owing to Scotland's close ties with France. Scottish royal palaces followed French court practice rather than that of England.

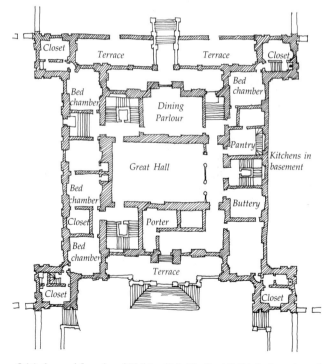

Original ground-floor plan of Wollaton Hall. The Great Hall is in the centre and entered by a circuitous route from the main entrance.

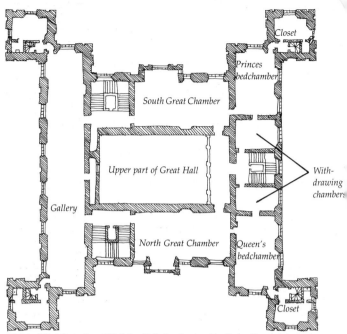

Original first-floor plan of Wollaton Hall showing two identical suites of state apartments.

There are surviving ranges of Tudor apartments of state and family apartments at Hardwick Hall in Derbyshire, a courtier-house built as a dynastic power base for the Countess of Shrewsbury ('Bess of Hardwick') by Robert Smythson in 1590-7. An example of a less grand range of apartments is to be found at Chastleton in Oxfordshire, attributed to Smythson and built in 1603-14 for a wealthy wool merchant. This family entertained local knights and worthies (who expected the honour of these apartments) but were never grand enough to entertain the Court – which is not what the builder aspired to, being outside the Court circle. These grand apartments were decorated with motifs culled from pattern books but not understood. The classical orders might or might not be correct and it took another hundred years before there was a true understanding of them.

The classical style that replaced the Gothic has enjoyed periods of popularity and rejection but is still with us today. Why should an architectural style evolved 3,000 years ago by the Greeks in the

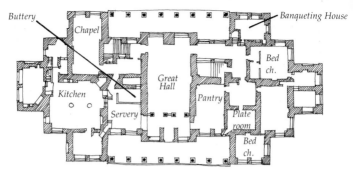

Original ground-floor plan of Hardwick Hall, Derbyshire, built 1590-7 by Smythson. The transverse Great Hall with buttery and pantry either side permitted a symmetrical façade with central entrance.

Mediterranean have been so enduring? The basic principle of Greek architecture is simply that of post-and-lintel, that is to say, of upright columns supporting horizontal beams, or lintels, and this monumental architecture was applied to Greek temples and public buildings. The Greeks also evolved a series of logical mathematical proportions for their posts, or columns, and devised three forms of decoration (as well as technical names) for the various parts of the column and the beam, or entablature. The three types of column, or 'order', are the Doric, the Corinthian and the Ionic. It was the Romans, who overrun the Greeks, who carried architecture much further and added two more orders to the original three, Tuscan and Composite, each with its own distinctive capital.

The five orders are given an ascending rank according to their height. The least important, stubbiest and simplest order, the Tuscan, has a column height of six times its diameter at the lower part of the shaft and little decoration. This is followed by the Doric, the oldest order. The Greek Doric had twenty flutings on the shaft and no base; the Romans added a base, made the capital less simple and the column itself higher, seven diameters instead of six. The third of the classical orders is the Ionic originating in Asia Minor in the sixth century B.C. Its most distinguishing feature is the capital decorated with four projecting volutes; the column is sometimes decorated with twenty-four flutings and has a height of nine times the base diameter. The fourth order is Corinthian with a very ornate capital of sprouting acanthus leaves and a height of ten diameters. The final, and Roman, order is the Composite, a mixture of Ionic and Corinthian and, like the Corinthian, is ten diameters in height. Used correctly, the orders should appear on a building in the right sequence. The entrance of the Old Bodleian Library, Oxford, has all five orders one above the other and in the correct sequence – even if four of the bases are incorrect.

THE CLASSICAL ORDERS

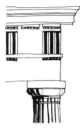

Greek Doric   *Ionic*   *Corinthian*

Tuscan   *Roman Doric*   *Composite*

The actual rules for the orders were worked out by the Romans and not the Greeks and they utilized the orders in ways the Greeks would not have dreamed of doing. In their architecture the Romans not only used the full round columns on their buildings but also invented square columns, or pilasters, and half-columns, called 'attached' columns. The Romans established spacings between the columns for all five orders, from one-and-a-half diameters for Doric to four for Corinthian and Composite, so achieving a perfect rhythm. Fortunately, these Roman principles and practices were recorded by the Roman architect Marcus Vitruvius Pollio whose *De Architectura* is the only complete architectural treatise to survive from Antiquity. Although to his contemporaries Vitruvius was of slight importance, his treatise first published in Rome in 1486, was immensely important for architects from the Early Renaissance onwards. The first to codify the five orders was Sebastiano Serlio (1475-1554), an Italian architect and painter who published *L'Architettura* in six parts between 1537 and 1551. The book was practical rather than theoretical and filled a need. Serlio went to France to advise on the building of Fontainebleau and his influence on French style was considerable. Serlio's book was widely circulated in England but little understood.

The Old Bodleian Library (1613-24), Oxford. An object lesson in five Classical orders beginning, correctly, at the bottom with Tuscan, followed by Doric, Ionic, Corinthian and finally Composite.

Andrea Palladio, the Venetian architect who died in 1580, built many villas in the Veneto for Venetian merchants and had an enormous influence on architecture in Britain, though only after his death, through his *Quattro libri dell'architettura*, published in 1570. Palladio knew the work of Vitruvius and applied his understanding to his buildings. Until excavations at Herculaneum and Pompeii began in 1708 there was little idea of what a Roman domestic house was like and the only Roman remains Palladio had to guide him were monumental buildings and tombs. Understandably, Palladio gave his patrons villas based on the Roman triumphal and religious architecture remaining above ground. The Villa Capra at Vicenza, called the 'Rotonda', has a Roman temple portico on each of its four fronts. Lord Burlington in 1724 adapted the design for his villa at Chiswick attached to the subsequently demolished Jacobean Chiswick House. A domed villa with a cool central hall attracting any of the four winds through its porticoes, as the Villa Capra was designed to do, is very practical for the hot summers of the Veneto; but, when such a building is transferred to the cold English winter countryside, it requires much modern heating and draught-proofing to counteract Palladio's air-conditioning. Still, the Villa Capra was repeated in England four times. There are now only two left standing, Mereworth Castle in Kent (not open to the public) and Chiswick Villa. The Palladian style, classical Roman architecture at second hand, was only established in Britain at the beginning of the eighteenth century, as we shall see in the next section.

The first architect to translate the Italian Renaissance style into England successfully was Inigo Jones who visited Italy in 1613 and returned with a copy of Palladio's *Quattro libri*. It survives in Worcester College library, Oxford, with notes by Jones in the margins. His first building was the Queen's House, at Greenwich begun in

The Queen's House, Greenwich (1616-35). The first 'Palladian' building in England, and Inigo Jones's earliest surviving building, based on the Palazzo Chericati, Vicenza, begun by Palladio in 1550.

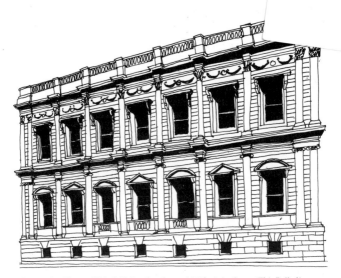

Banqueting House, Whitehall, London, begun 1619 by Inigo Jones. This Palladian prototype must have presented a startling contrast to the jumble of medieval and Elizabethan buildings surrounding it.

1616 but, owing to the death of Queen Anne in 1619, not completed until 1637. The building is an adaptation of Palladio's Palazzo Chiericati in Vicenza, begun in 1550. Jones's second building was the Banqueting House, Whitehall, begun in 1619 as part of an unachieved and ambitious rebuilding of the Palace of Whitehall.

In Scotland the Renaissance was accepted rather more readily than in England. At Stirling Castle James III (1460-88) built the great hall designed by Robert Cochrane. This was one of the first and finest fifteenth-century buildings anywhere in Britain. At Falkland Palace the north façade of the courtyard (1539-42) is purely French. But then its builder, James V (1513-42), had married the daughter of François I. James V also completed the great palace block at Stirling begun by James IV (1473-1513) with French masons. Heriot's Hospital, Edinburgh, begun in 1628 by William Wallace is a grand expression of Scottish taste and almost baroque in style with triangular window heads – a Scottish fashion since the time of James V. Wallace may also have been responsible for part of Linlithgow Palace built in 1619-20.

Although the floor plans of the grander houses built in this period were inevitably tied to the past, in the smaller houses there was a dramatic change in the sixteenth century. The hall plan remained

Stirling Castle, Central Region. The Hall block (1460-88) is by Robert Cochrane and one of first and finest Renaissance buildings in Britain.

Falkland Palace, Fife Region'. The courtyard facade built 1537-41 has a strong French flavour; an early Renaissance influence without parallel in Britain.

Heriot's Hospital, Edinburgh, begun in 1617. The building is symmetrical around a courtyard and is an early herald of the coming of Scottish baroque.

universal in both great and smaller houses. However, in the smaller properties the fire, previously burning on a central hearth or in a fireplace on a side wall, was moved to a central stack with two back-to-back hearths between the hall and the parlour. This had the advantage of keeping all the heat within the four walls of the dwelling. The earliest surviving building with this feature is a small hunting lodge in Sherwood Forest, built in 1522-37 for Lord Hussey. This lodge, created for the relaxation of the Chief Butler of England, has terracotta brickwork that may have come from Hampton Court Palace which was Hussey's responsibility when Henry VIII was completing the building. This central-stack plan with entrance door opening into a small lobby against the central chimney and a staircase on the other side, became standard for most smaller houses by 1600 and remained in fashion for the rest of the seventeenth century. This innovation was not taken up by the builders of the courtier-houses. The old-fashioned hall plan with screens passage gave scope for displays of pageantry and power by the wealthy. Audley End in Essex, built for the Earl of Suffolk in 1605-14 and originally twice its present size, has an ornate screen decorated with strap-work with the service rooms behind it. Hatfield House, Hertford-

The reconstructed facade of Kneesall Old Hall, Nottinghamshire, a hunting lodge built 1522-37 for Lord Hussey, Chief Butler of England, the earliest example of a central stack plan with a back-to-back chimney.

FIRST FLOOR
Chamber.

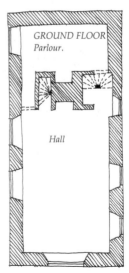

GROUND FLOOR
Parlour.

Hall

shire, begun in 1607 for Lord Salisbury has a similar layout. However, Holland House, Kensington, built in 1606-7 for Sir Walter Cope, a friend of Salisbury's, which had an entrance hall and no great hall, was a forerunner of a more convenient plan. The house was, alas, bombed in 1941.

For the first time what were later known as 'follies' were built during this period. They were a rich man's indulgence, Sir Thomas Tresham, a Roman Catholic, spent his money on building statements of his religious belief on his Northamptonshire estate; the Triangular Lodge at Rushton (1594) represents a pun on the Holy Trinity. More conventionally, he started, but never finished, Lyveden New Bield (c.1600). In Derbyshire at Bolsover Castle, Sir Charles Cavendish, youngest son of Bess of Hardwick, in a fit of romanticism, rebuilt a Norman motte and bailey castle. Begun in 1612, it must surely be the first example of Gothic Revival style. Bolsover was a play-house ten miles from his great mansion, Welbeck Abbey, and never intended for continuous occupation.

The Triangular Lodge, Rushton, Northamptonshire. An early folly, built by Sir Thomas Tresham in 1594-7 as a symbol of the Trinity and his Catholic faith.

Bolsover Castle, Derbyshire, begun 1612 by Smythson for Sir Charles Cavendish, is an early example of Romantic Gothic Revival.

Typical Features of Tudor and Jacobean Houses

Plan: Common to all types of dwelling was the hall, house-place or housebody, entered at the end of one of the longer sides. In larger houses a screen formed an entrance passage. Kitchens and services of pantry and buttery were invariably placed on the north and north-west away from the prevailing wind. Access to the services was from the screens passage. The early Tudor courtier-houses were built to an H-plan (with the hall in the cross-bar) and with gatehouse and enclosed courtyard. Later, the plan changed to the E-type in which the hall entrance was by a porch in the centre bar of the E. This plan had nothing to do with the Queen's initial letter. As the century progressed Renaissance symmetry demanded a less irregular elevation and Wollaton Hall, Hardwick Hall and others, mainly the works of Smythson, were built to geometrical plans with porters' lodges and walled forecourts replacing the earlier gatehouses and courtyards. Often strategically placed on a hill top, courtier-houses express power and patronage. Long galleries, originally called galleries, are found in the larger houses on an upper floor looking down on garden parterres. The galleries were secondary rooms of reception, a step down from state apartments and used, too, for exercise and privacy away from family rooms.

Elevation: Stone was the preferred building material; at Wollaton Hall, the stone faced on a brick core, the stone was brought from thirty miles away. Where stone was not available, brick was increasingly used. To decorate blank exterior walls, diaper patterns and other designs were made in brickwork by using the blackened heads of over-baked bricks or, in flint walls, flint. In the first half of the sixteenth century walls tended to be flat; but from the time of Longleat

Smythson used projecting square turrets to buttress high walls weakened by large window openings.

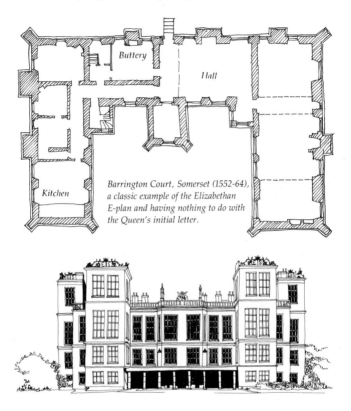

Barrington Court, Somerset (1552-64), a classic example of the Elizabethan E-plan and having nothing to do with the Queen's initial letter.

Buttery

Hall

Kitchen

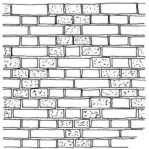

Above: Hardwick Hall, Derbyshire. A symmetrical facade conceals a medieval floor-plan. Built 1590-7 by Smythson, the building was a power-base for the dynasty of Bess of Hardwick.

Left: A typical Tudor brick decoration using the over-baked heads of bricks in a diaper pattern.

Roof: Chimneys and the shapes they could be built in fascinated the Tudors. Fluted, twisted, and crenelated they create fantastic silhouettes to buildings. Later, the Gothic designs of the early chimneys gave way to more classical columns topped with entablatures. Wollaton Hall (1588) had these but they have lost their entablatures. Small banqueting houses with domes added further exciting features to roof lines. At Longleat there are eight such banqueting houses and Burghley has a collection of them with pepper-pot tops. Gable ends were decorated with strapwork and shaped with curves. Blickling Hall, Norfolk (1616-25), and Montacute, Somerset (1590s), are two with shaped gables. In smaller houses roofs were steep, clay tiled or thatched.

Interior: Much colour from tapestries and painted plasterwork. In the first half of the sixteenth century the decoration was heraldic and flat but by 1600 moulded plasterwork on overmantels, friezes of figures and scenes taken from woodcuts were fashionable. In family rooms decoration consisted of family heraldry but in state apartments the heraldry was royal.

Hardwick Hall, Derbyshire. The extravagance of huge windows weakening the walls was counteracted by the buttresses of the projecting towers. The letters ES on the roof stand for Elizabeth Shrewsbury (Bess of Hardwick) the builder.

Windows: Became larger and are another expression of wealth and power. Expanses of glass were not cheap; they were also draughty. The total cost of the glass in the vast windows at Hardwick Hall was probably around £1000 or one-eighth of the whole building cost. Oriel windows (bay windows on upper floors) were used throughout this period.

Gardens: Geometrical shapes were popular in the Renaissance garden, although not one has survived. Nature was constrained to man's will and unnatural straight lines, angles and even strapwork were used in parterres, i.e. low hedging around beds filled with coloured flowers and even coloured stones and broken brick. Galleries overlooked the parterre garden.

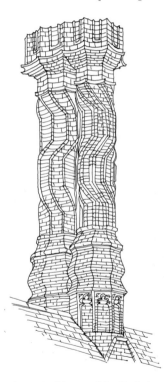

Elizabethan builders delighted in the Gothic shapes they devised for chimneys. After 1580 they used Classical columns and pediments.

Some Architects of the Period

Robert Smythson (1536-1614): To use the term architect is misleading. Plans, elevations and details were provided by masons. However, on his memorial Smythson is described as 'Architector' and he was the first to be so described. The only building ascribed to him with certainty is Wollaton Hall (1580-8), Nottingham. Other buildings, such as Hardwick Hall (1590-7), Derbyshire, and Bolsover Castle (1612-27), Derbyshire, completed by his son John (d. 1634), are ascribed to him stylistically and by evidence of payments. Smythson was a genius in managing space and the state apartments at Hardwick Hall are magical. His skill at devising many different floor levels is shown at Bolsover Castle.

Robert Stickells (d. 1620): Like Smythson he was a mason but records show him acting as an architect. He was employed by Sir Thomas Tresham and it is likely that he had a hand in the design of Lyveden New Bield, and other works commissioned by Tresham in and around Rushton, Northamptonshire.

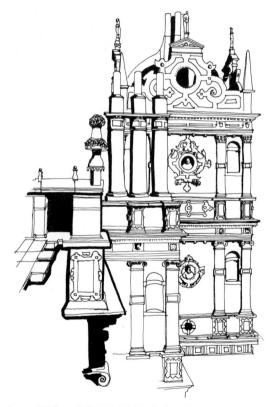

Roofscape of Wollaton Hall (1580-88), Nottingham. The ornate turret crowned with strapwork was a roof banqueting house. The chimneys of Classical columns were topped with entablatures.

Blickling Hall, Norfolk, built 1616-25. The entrance front has three Dutch gables and moderate strapwork over third-floor windows.

Cybele, goddess of plenty: a plaster overmantel at Hardwick Hall (1590-7), Derbyshire, represents a complement to Queen Elizabeth I and would have been polychrome.

Where to See Examples

North – ***Burton Agnes Hall*** (B.A.H. Preservation Trust Ltd), nr Bridlington, Humberside, tall, brick building with stone trim 1610, attributed to Smythson, great hall, parlour and great chamber; ***Burton Constable*** (Mr. J. Chichester Constable), nr Hull, Humberside, brick with stone trim, exterior of 1600, interior C18; ***Levens Hall*** (Mr C.H. Bagot) nr Kendall, Cumbria, Elizabethan manor with fine plasterwork and panelling, after 1578.

Midlands – ***Bolsover Castle*** (EH), Derbyshire, begun 1612 by Smythson in Gothic Revival style; ***Cannons Ashby*** (NT), Northamptonshire, brick and stone manor house of *c.*1580 last altered in 1710, Elizabethan wall decoration and Jacobean plasterwork; ***Chastleton House*** (Mrs. Clutton-Brock), Oxfordshire, tall manor house attributed to Smythson *c.*1603; **Cwmmau Farmhouse** (NT), Hereford and Worcester, early C17 timber-framed; ***Hardwick Hall*** (NT), Derbyshire, begun 1590 by Smythson for Bess of Hardwick, complete set of apartments both family and state – the least altered of the Elizabethan courtier-houses; ***Kirby Hall*** (EH), nr Corby, Northamptonshire, extraordinary courtyard building with strong French influence begun 1570, garden being restored; ***Lyveden New Bield*** (NT), Northamptonshire, unfinished and unusual *c.*1600; ***Old House Museum*** (Bakewell Hist. Soc.), Bakewell, Derbyshire, Tudor house with screens passage and open chamber; ***Sulgrave Manor*** (Sulgrave Manor Board), Banbury, Northamptonshire, small manor

An oriel at Montacute House (1590s), Somerset, lights the Gallery running the length of the top floor.

of 1558, home of ancestors of George Washington; **Triangular Lodge** (EH), Rushton, Northamptonshire, symbolic of the Holy Trinity built 1594; **Wollaton Hall** (City of Nottingham), Nottingham, astonishing exterior by Smythson 1580-8, little of the original interior.

South – **Charlton House** (London B. of Greenwich), Charlton, Greenwich, SE7., brick with stone trim 1607; **Corsham Court** (Ld Methuen), Chippenham, Wiltshire, south front Smythson (att.) 1582; **Godinton Place** (Mr A. Wyndham Green), Ashford, Kent, main front 1620s hiding earlier timber-framed building, great hall and great chamber; **Haremere Hall** (Ly Killearn), Etchington, East Sussex, symmetrical Jacobean, great hall 1610; **Knole** (NT), Sevenoaks, Kent, vast house with 17 courtyards built 1456-1608, great hall, parlour and great chambers; **Lacock Abbey** (NT), nr Chippenham, Wiltshire, C13 abbey converted into a house in 1540 has two stone Renaissance tables, one in a roof banqueting house; **Longleat House** (M. of Bath), Warminster, Wiltshire, earliest survivor of the English

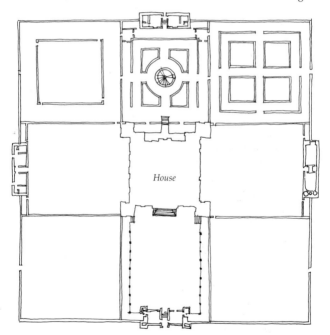

Smythson's plan for a geometrical Renaissance garden at Wollaton Hall (1580-8), Nottingham, the earliest surviving plan of this type in which the garden is an extension of the house. The circular device was a fountain-sundial.

Renaissance, built by French architect and mason Alan Maynard in 1570 and Smythson in 1567, of the original interior only the great hall survives; **Losely Park** (Mr J.R. More-Molyneux), nr Guildford, Surrey, great hall, parlour and great chamber 1562-8, but gallery demolished in 1835; **Old Wardour Castle** (EH), nr Shaftsbury, Wiltshire, C14 castle modernised by Smythson in 1578, towers on the entrance front were often repeated by Smythson, now a roofless ruin; **Parham House** (Hon. C. & Mrs Gibson), Pulborough, West Sussex, great parlour and great chamber, begun 1577.

Old Wardour Castle, Wiltshire. The entrance, flanked by two massive towers, was a feature copied many times by Smythson, who worked here in 1578 modernizing a medieval castle.

South-West – Barrington Court (NT), Somerset, the perfect example of the E-plan, built before 1530 and restored early C20; **Cotehele** (NT), nr Saltash, Cornwall, great hall, parlour and great chamber, late C15; **Montacute House** (NT), Yeovil, Somerset, great hall, parlour and great chamber, begun in 1590s; **Sand** (Lt Col. P.V. Huyshe), nr Sidmouth, Devon, manor house rebuilt 1592-4, great hall with screens passage; **Trerice** (NT), nr Newquay, Cornwall, great hall and great chamber 1572.

Scotland – *Castle Menzies* (Menzies Clan Soc.), Tayside Region, elongated Z-plan 1577; *Craigievar* (NTS), Grampian Region, supreme example of L-plan tower-house 1610-26; *Crathes Castle* (NTS), Grampian Region, tower-house c.1553-c.1595; *Culross Palace* (SSS), Fife Region, 1597 and 1611; *Edzell Castle Garden* (SSS), Tayside Region, the castle is ruined but an early C17 formal garden survives; *Falkland Palace* (H.M. the Queen), Fife Region, courtyard façades in French Renaissance style 1537-41; *Linlithgow Palace* (SSS), Lothian Region, ruined birth-place of Mary Queen of Scots, the section built in Scottish Renaissance style 1619-20 is possibly by William Wallace; *Muchalls Castle* (Mr M.A. Simpson), Grampian Region, L-plan house 1607-27; *Stirling Castle* (SSS), Central Region, great hall by Robert Cochrane, the finest C15 Renaissance building in Britain; *Winton House* (SSS), Lothian Region, earlier house enlarged by Wm. Wallace 1620-7.

Wales – *Plas Teg* (Mrs C. Bayley), 1610, nr Mold, Clwyd, fine Jacobean building; *Plas Mawr* (Royal Conway Academy of Art), Conwy, Gwynedd, built 1577-80 by a diplomat who had lived in Flanders.

THE AGE OF INIGO JONES 1620-60

When Jones returned from his last visit to Italy in 1615 he was appointed Surveyor of the King's Works. As surveyor, he was fully occupied not only with architecture but also with designing masques, or theatricals, for the Queen and interior decoration for the Royal palaces. Although some private buildings are attributed to Jones, it is unlikely that he had the time for many private commissions. It was left to his devotees to fill the gap.

In 1636 Isaac de Caux, a Frenchman in Jones's drawing office, began a projected major rebuilding of Wilton House in Wiltshire – Jones had refused the commission owing to his work at Greenwich. Only the south wing of Wilton was ever built; it was gutted by fire in 1647 and restored by John Webb, a pupil and assistant to Jones.

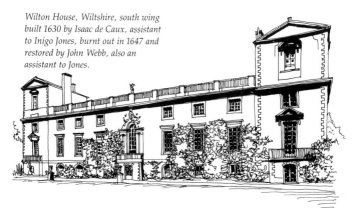

Wilton House, Wiltshire, south wing built 1630 by Isaac de Caux, assistant to Inigo Jones, burnt out in 1647 and restored by John Webb, also an assistant to Jones.

After the restoration of Wilton, Webb went on to build the central section of Lamport Hall, Northamptonshire, in 1654-7 (the wings are later) and, about the same time, added a portico to The Vyne in Hampshire. This was the first classical portico on a private house in Britain.

Unfortunately Jones was not followed to Italy by other architects and his message was not understood. There were too few of his buildings to set a trend. The Civil War came in 1642 and it was only in 1650 that another house was built in the classical style at Coleshill in Berkshire by an amateur architect, Sir Roger Pratt. Coleshill was completed in 1662 but no longer exists; it was burnt down in 1952.

The *piano nobile* at Coleshill was raised over basement services containing the kitchen, etc. and entered by a short flight of steps leading into an imposing entrance hall with a grand staircase. Directly behind the hall was the great parlour, or saloon, with a withdrawing room while to the left of the hall, on the south side, were two bedchambers with antechambers. One of them, the principal chamber for important visitors, had a closet as well – the complete layout of a French apartment. A cupola gave access to a flat roof-walk surrounded by a balustrade. Coleshill was a 'double pile' house, i.e. two rooms deep. This plan and exterior became a standard for the Baroque period 1660-1720.

Lamport Hall, Northamptonshire. The centre five bays comprise the house built 1654-7 by John Webb. The wings were added later by Francis Smith of Warwick in 1732-8. The central pediment is nineteenth century.

As Coleshill was being constructed, another house with a similar exterior, Thorpe Hall, Cambridgeshire, was being built (1653-6) by Peter Mills. Even at this late date there was still a hall, screens passage and services on the ground floor. Thorpe Hall, alas, is not open to the public but easily visible from the very busy main road to Peterborough. Scandalously neglected by the local authority that owns the building, it is still recognisably very influenced by Coleshill.

Whereas the classical style appealed to only a few in England, what is called the 'Artisan style' supplied a common need for the majority. The 'Dutch House' (Kew Palace) in Kew Gardens, begun

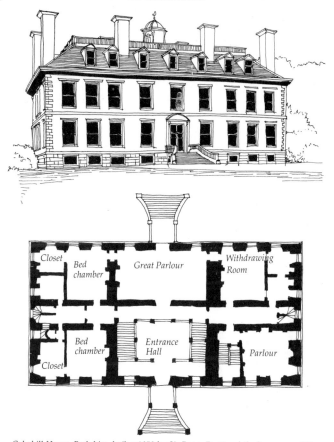

Coleshill House, Berkshire, built c.1650 by Sir Roger Pratt and the forerunner of the standard Baroque house. Unfortunately Coleshill was burnt down in 1952.

1631 and so called because of its Dutch gables, is built entirely in brick although the details of pilasters, string courses and window surrounds derive from building in stone. Raynham Hall, in Norfolk, was built *c.*1635 by Sir Roger Townshend who took the trouble to take his mason to France. Consequently the building is more advanced than the Dutch House. Although is is built of brick, the details are in stone and the plan owes much to Palladio.

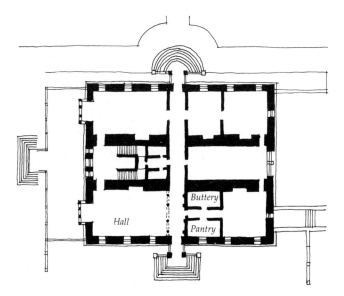

Thorpe Hall (1653-6), Cambridgeshire. The exterior owes much to Coleshill but the interior still has the old-fashioned plan of Great Hall and services.

The 'Dutch House' (Kew Palace) at Kew, London, begun 1631 in the 'Artisan style'. A style for those who were apprehensive of the Palladian architecture introduced by Inigo Jones.

Raynham Hall (c.1635), Norfolk, owes a debt to Palladianism. The builder, Sir Roger Townsend, took his mason to France and consequently Raynham is far more advanced than the 'Dutch House'.

In smaller houses, the yeoman farmer continued to feed his family and farm workers in his hall, but living-in servants were accommodated in attic rooms. This practice necessitates a higher roof profile to these buildings and some roofs were heightened and steepened to accommodate the attic dormitories. The convenient form of the central stack with back-to-back hearths became more widespread and the room space behind the stack became a kitchen in the more pretentious dwellings. The old open halls were ceiled over to give more upper-floor accommodation.

Useful Dates
By the mid seventeenth century brick was increasingly popular. English bond gave way to Flemish bond which used alternating headers and stretchers; it was more economical but less strong, generally held to have been first used at the Dutch House, Kew in 1631. From the mid seventeenth century the roof-walk with balustrade and cupola became almost a standard feature of greater houses. Classical columns, pediments and 'Venetian', or 'Serlian', windows, became an increasingly fashionable hallmark of Palladian origins.

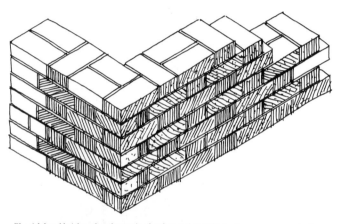

Flemish bond brickwork – alternating headers and stretchers – became very popular by mid-seventeenth century and first used at Kew in 1631.

Some Architects of the Period
Inigo Jones (1573-1652): He brought to England the first understanding of classical architecture. Unfortunately, he was a man before his time and his genius was not appreciated for another 100 years. The Queen's House (1616-35), Greenwich, London, SW10, and the Banqueting House (1619-22), Whitehall, SW1, are the first true classical buildings in England and based on Jones's study of Palladio's villas in the Veneto. There is evidence of his involvement in the design of the south front of Wilton House, Wiltshire. Otherwise, all Jones's fully authenticated buildings have been demolished. On the authority of Colen Campbell he is credited with the remaining pavilion at Stoke Park, Northamptonshire.
John Webb (1611-72): A pupil and nephew by marriage of Inigo

Jones, he had the misfortune to be born in the time of the Civil War which prevented royal patronage and private building until the 1660s. Webb was responsible for the reconstruction of the interior of the south front of Wilton House, Wiltshire, after a serious fire in 1647. He designed the classical portico for The Vyne, Hampshire, in 1654-6, and the centre block of Lamport Hall, Northamptonshire, in 1655-7. At the restoration of the Monarchy he was commissioned to build a new palace at Greenwich in 1664-9 but only the Charles II block was completed by Webb.

Where to See Examples
London – *Banqueting House*, Inigo Jones 1619-22, Whitehall, SW1; *Queen's House*, Inigo Jones 1616-19, Greenwich, SE17.

A 'Serlian' or 'Venetian' window of three lights, a hallmark of Palladian origins and incidentally very difficult to hang curtains on.

North – *Temple Newsam House* (Leeds Metro. DC), West Yorkshire, brick with stone trim 1622-37.

Midlands – *Bridgnorth Town Hall*, Shropshire, 1648-52; *Kirby Hall* (EH), Northamptonshire, part by Nicholas Stone 1638-40; *Lilford Hall* (Mr J.M. Dishington), nr Oundle, Northamptonshire, Jacobean c.1630.

East – *Felbrigg Hall* (NT), Norfolk, south front c.1620; **Cambridge**: *Christ's College*, Fellows' Building 1640-3; *Clare College*, East Range J. Westley 1638-40, West Range c.1640, South Range 1640-2; *Old Court* (Brick Building), 1633-4.

South-West – *Lanhydrock House* (NT), nr Bodmin, Cornwall, a great house begun 1630, burnt out in 1881 and rebuilt, only the original gallery survives; *Wilton House* (E. of Pembroke), Salisbury, Wiltshire, east wing exterior begun in 1630, interior burnt in 1647 recreated 1649 by John Webb.

Scotland – *Culross Town House* (NTS), Fife Region, 1626 altered 1783; *Heriot's Hospital*, Edinburgh, begun 1628 by William Wallace, magnificent building, almost baroque; *House of the Binns* (NTS), by Linlithgow, Central Region, 1621-30, good plaster ceilings.

CHURCH BUILDING 1530-1660

Up to the accession of Queen Elizabeth in 1558 there had been virtually no church building at all since the breach with Rome and little enough even up to 1660. Some 6,000 medieval churches served a population of around 3.5 million in the 1550s. Old churches were adapted to Protestant worship by destroying or covering images and wall paintings, but screens were in general preserved. In the 1630s Archbishop Laud felt that the exposure of the altar lacked reverence – before this the congregation took Communion, as if at the Last Supper, kneeling around a table in the chancel. Laud had the wooden altar-tables moved back to the east wall and rails installed to keep away dogs; the congregation took Communion kneeling at the rail. Box pews in oak survive from this period as well as triple-decker pulpits.

Inigo Jones began classicizing the exterior of St Paul's Cathedral in London in 1633. At the same time, St Katherine Cree, London, consecrated in 1631, was still Gothic with only a passing nod to classicism in the arches and columns of the aisles. Of great consequence is Jones's church of St Paul, Covent Garden, built in 1631 in a strict classical style with a Tuscan portico, the first of its kind in England. St John's at Groombridge, Kent, built 1625 and St John's, Leeds, of 1632-3, are other rare examples of new churches for this period but even rarer are churches built during the Commonwealth; Plaxtol, Kent, is one, built in 1649 and enlarged in 1852. Staunton Harold church, Leicestershire, was built 1653 in the old Gothic style by Sir Robert Shirley as an act of defiance against the Puritans who had banned the Prayer Book; he died in the Tower in 1656 for his pains. The church has been little altered and its original fitting and communion plate are intact.

The Chapel, Haddon Hall, Derbyshire, is furnished with enclosed box pews and a triple-decker pulpit all in oak and dated 1632. Traces of original paint colours still survive.

Where to See Examples

(arranged alphabetically by place names)

London – *St Giles*, Cripplegate, EC2, restored after bomb damage in World War Two; *Queen's Chapel*, St James's Palace, SW1, the first classical church in England by Inigo Jones 1623-30; *St Paul's*, Covent Garden, WC2, Inigo Jones 1631-8, *St Luke*, Charlton, Greenwich, SE7, c.1630, brick, *St John*, Church Road, Maldon, brick early C17; *St Lawrence*, Morden Park, 1638; *St John*, Stanmore, brick 1630s; *St Katherine Cree*, Leadenhall Street, EC3, 1628-31.

St Paul's church, Covent Garden, London, built by Inigo Jones in 1631 in a strict Classical style. The Tuscan portico was the first of its kind in England.

North – Holy Trinity, **Berwick-on-Tweed**, Northumberland, J. Young 1648-52; Old St Leonard Church, **Billington, Lancashire,** *c.*1577; St Mary Magdalene, **Broughton-in-Furness**, Cumbria, consecrated 1547, later additions; St John, **Leeds**, West Yorkshire, 1632-3; Holy Trinity, **Rivington**, Lancashire, *c.*1540, remodelled *c.*1666; St Wilfred, **Standish**, Greater Manchester, rebuilt 1582-4.

Midlands – St Peter, **Broughton**, Staffordshire, Gothic style with box-pews 1630-4; St Wilfred, **Grappenhall**, Cheshire, rebuilt 1525-39; St Peter, **Hargrave**, Cheshire, 1627; All Saints, **Harthill**, Cheshire, *c.*1609; St Nicholas, **Holcot**, Bedfordshire, 1590; St Mary, **Leighton Bromswold**, Cambridgeshire, 1626-34; Metheringham Church, **Lincolnshire**, *c.*1600; Brasenose College Chapel, **Oxford**, J. Jackson (att.) 1656; All Saints, **Risley**, Derbyshire, 1593; Staunton Harold, **Leicestershire**, another of the few, by R. Shepherd 1653-63.

East – St James (now cathedral), **Bury St Edmunds**, Suffolk, 1510-1550s; Peterhouse College Chapel, **Cambridge**, 1632; St Michael, **Woodham Walter**, Essex, brick 1563-4.

South – St Peter, **Buntingford**, Hertfordshire, brick 1614-16; St Mary, **Chiddingstone**, Kent, rebuilt after fire 1625-9; St John, **Groombridge**, Kent, 1625; St Nicholas, **North Stoneham**, Hampshire, 1590-1610; Plaxtol Church, **Kent**, one of few built during the Commonwealth; St Nicholas, **Rochester**, Kent, rebuilt 1624; St Nicholas, **Shepperton**, Surrey, flint 1614; St Michael, **South Malling**, East Sussex, 1626-8; St James, **Southwick**, Hampshire, rebuilt 1566.

South-West – Holy Trinity, *Cold Aston*, Avon, rebuilt 1508-40; St Lawrence, *Folke*, Dorset, rebuilt 1628; St Andrew, *Munterne Magna*, Dorset, *c.*1610-20; Holy Trinity, *Wyke Champflower*, Somerset, 1623-4.

Scotland – *Anstruther Easter*, Fife Region, simple barrel-vaulted church, built after 1636; St Columba, *Burntisland*, Fife Region, striking square plan with central tower 1592; *Dirleton Church*, Lothian Region, 1612; Tron Kirk, *Edinburgh*, J. Mylne 1637-47, partially rebuilt 1824; *Fordell Chapel*, Fife Region, Gothic style 1650; St Mary, *Grandtully*, Tayside Region, early C16, painted ceiling 1636; *Kirkmaiden Church*, Dumfries & Galloway Region, 1638; *Pittenweem*, Fife Region, 1588, tower and spire *c.*1630; *Tibbermore Church*, Tayside Region, 1632, enlarged, 1810.

CHRISTOPHER WREN AND THE BAROQUE 1660-1720

The Baroque style is characterized by exuberant decoration, expansive, curvaceous forms and a delight in large-scale, sweeping vistas. It is also theatrical and appeals to the emotions. The term applies to seventeenth-century art and architecture in Italy and to the seventeenth and early eighteenth centuries in Spain, Germany and Austria. France was less affected by Baroque, while in Britain Baroque was a watered down affair in comparison with the effects achieved in Italy and southern Austria. Deception is at the heart of the style; nothing is what it seems, billowing curtains turn out to be made of plaster, and marble to be painted wood.

In Britain, Baroque was used by the Court and Court circles to create grandiose architecture and interiors overwhelming the observer with a sense of the power and wealth of the personage at the centre. Unlike other art forms Baroque was a way of life in the English court circle; Baroque music, theatre, painting, clothes and even a Baroque style of living distinguishes this period. In Britain it had a very short run.

With the restoration of the monarchy in 1660 the door was at last open to the mainstream of French influence; after long years of exile in France and the Netherlands the Court was familiar with the latest ideas in architecture. Returning Royalists had run up debts abroad and their estates, confiscated by the Commonwealth, had to be reclaimed. This all took time and little private building was undertaken until the 1670s. There was no similar constraint for Charles II or the colleges at Oxford and Cambridge. As early as 1662 there was an ambitious plan of building a new palace at Greenwich to designs by John Webb and never completed; the Naval Hospital was designed thirty years later by Christopher Wren. Pembroke College chapel (1663-5), Cambridge; the Sheldonian Theatre, Oxford (1664-9), and Emmanuel College chapel, Cambridge (1668-73), are all by Wren. It was Christopher Wren (1632-1723), Surveyor-General of the Royal Works who left his indelible mark on the period; St Paul's Cathedral and fifty London churches were rebuilt by him and his associates after the Great Fire of 1666.

The span of sixty years from 1660 to 1720 saw the evolution and death of the Baroque style in Britain. Baroque was not a strong influence in the French Court which partly explains why the style took a different course in Britain from that developed in Italy. Hampton Court Palace, partly rebuilt by Wren in 1690-6, is an echo of Versailles and its gardens – Wren had visited France in 1665 and had seen the Versailles of Le Vau with its gardens by Le Nôtre. The fashion set by the Court was followed by its courtiers. Vast Baroque houses were built, such as Castle Howard, Yorkshire, by Vanbrugh, completed in 1726, and Blenheim Palace, Oxfordshire, begun by Vanbrugh but completed by Hawksmoor in 1725. However, the Crown had lost its absolute power to Parliament and the King no longer travelled with his ministers; the vast Baroque palaces designed to accommodate Court and government were outdated when completed. They express the dying ambitions of the Stuart Court; their builders created extravagant backgrounds for monarchs who seldom held court beneath their roofs. Instead of building for a monarch, courtiers now built for themselves and expressed their political power, wealth and influence through their buildings.

Hampton Court Palace, London: The rebuilding by Christopher Wren in 1690-6 was, with its gardens, based on Versailles which Wren saw in 1665.

TOWN HOUSES

The tradition of half-timbered town houses was effectively ended by the Rebuilding Acts of 1667 and 1707, requiring that buildings in

London should be of brick or stone and only permitting wood for windows, roof construction, cornices and doors. The Act of 1667 allowed four classes of house. The first sort, facing streets and lanes, were to be of two storeys, each 9ft in height. The second, superior type of dwelling fronting the Thames and the better streets, were allowed three storeys, the two lower ones 10ft high and the top one 9ft high. The third variety, built in the four principal London streets, were to be of four storeys, while the fourth, or best type of house standing in its own grounds, were also allowed four storeys. Windows and doorcases were to be fitted flush with the walls. Terraced houses in brick, originally introduced by Inigo Jones in Covent Garden as early as 1631, made an effective fire barrier and became a standard feature of the post-Fire rebuilding. The earliest surviving houses built after the Great Fire of 1666 are to be seen north of Fleet Street in Racquet Court and in Gough Square, where the house in which Dr Johnson later lived, No. 17, is an example.

The Act of 1707 went further and required windows and doorcases to be fitted 4in back from the face of the wall and prohibited wooden cornices and eaves. This last requirement had the effect of introducing the parapet wall at roof level. These regulations, although originating in the Stuart period, are taken to mark the change to Georgian style of town house and, while infallible for dating London houses, should be used with caution in provincial centres where the regulations were adopted at later dates.

In Scotland, the situation was very different. Medieval systems of landholding had resulted in small parcels of land in towns and the need to build high. There was also a French tradition of living in apartments: rich and poor shared the same tenements. In Edinburgh, Milne's Court, at the top of Lawnmarket, was built in 1690 by R. Mylne. It is a plain building of six storeys plus attic, built in stone with no decorative trim and with sash windows spaced in a splendid classical rhythm.

CHURCHES

As we have already seen, there was little building of churches before 1660. However, the Great Fire provided the urgent necessity for rebuilding London's churches. Inigo Jones had shown what could be done using classical proportions at St Paul's, Covent Garden. Changed liturgy affected church interiors and it was essential for the congregation to be able to see the altar, pulpit and lectern as well as to hear the service. These simple requirements were often impossible in the old layout of Gothic churches. Wren solved the problem by building churches that were, in effect, preaching boxes. The greater part of the fifty-two 'Wren' City churches were built to designs produced in the office of the Surveyor-General and not by Wren himself. Many buildings with a superficial resemblance to the 'Wren' style are attributed to him; apart from Inigo Jones, perhaps no other English architect is so falsely credited with buildings put up by others.

St Stephen's Walbrook,` London, built 1672-87 by Christopher Wren. The dome is a forerunner for that of St Paul's Cathedral.

Nicholas Hawksmoor (1660-1736), who worked in Wren's office and was associated with nearly all Wren's projects from *c*.1684 onwards, developed his own particular style. He was closely involved in building the fifty 'New City Churches in London' under the Act of 1711 as were James Gibbs (1682-1754), and Thomas Archer (1668-1743).

Scotland was slower to adopt the classical in church building, a style only fully developed by the 1750s.

Typical Features of 'Wren' Style Churches

Plan: Designed to fit some very awkward City sites but basically a hall often with galleries for bigger congregations. The entrance, where possible from the west end, was beneath a tower or, in later churches, a steeple.

Elevation: Two-storeyed with classical detail. Use of giant orders, pillared porticos and classical decoration on cornices. Large entrance doors, windows, often with rounded arches, on two levels with the larger one uppermost, plain glass and thin glazing bars.

Roof: Balustrading conceals a low pitch roof. Occasionally, a dome as at St Stephen Walbrook.

Interior: Light and uncluttered. Highly decorated plaster ceilings; carved woodwork, only very rarely by Grinling Gibbons, over the altar and on canopied pulpit; box pews.

Where to See Examples

London – Of the fifty-two churches designed by Wren's office almost all have been destroyed by bombs in World War II, demolished, altered or 'restored' by the Victorians. The following are relatively untouched: *St Benet's,* (now the Welsh Church) 1677-83, Paul's Wharf, EC4; *St James* 1676-83, Garlick Hill, EC4; *St Margaret Pattens* 1684-7, Eastcheap, EC3; *St Martin* 1677-84, Ludgate Hill, EC4; *St Michael* 1670-2, completed by Hawksmoor 1718-22, Cornhill, EC3; *St Stephen* 1672-9, has the St Paul's prototype dome, restored 1951-2 after bombing, Walbrook, EC4. The plasterer John Grove worked in all, and H. Doogood, also a plasterer, in all except St Michael's, Cornhill. Wren's masterpiece is St Paul's Cathedral 1675-1710.

Churches by Nicholas Hawksmoor (all altered in the C19): *Christ Church* 1714-29, Spitalfields, E1; *St George* 1716-31, Bloomsbury Way, WC1; *St Mary Woolnoth* 1716-24, Lombard Street, EC3.

Churches by James Gibbs: *St Mary-le-Strand* 1714-17, Strand, WC2; *St Peter* 1721-4, Vere Street, W1; *St Martin-in-the-Fields* 1722-6, Trafalgar Square, SW1.

Churches by Thomas Archer: *St John* 1713-28, Smith Square, SW1; *St Paul* 1713-30, Deptford.

Outside London (arranged alphabetically by place name):

North – St Aidan, *Billinge,* Merseyside, rebuilt 1718; *Handley Church*, Cheshire, 1662; *Knutsford*, Cheshire, Unitarian Meeting House, 1689; *Lowther Church*, Cumbria, remodelled 1686; *Maccles-*

St Paul's Cathedral, London, Christoper Wren's Classical masterpiece 1675-1710.

field, Cheshire, Unitarian Chapel, 1689; St Andrew, **Penrith,** Cumbria, 1720-2; Holy Trinity, **Sunderland,** Tyne & Wear, brick with stone trim 1719; St Helen, **Thorganby,** North Yorkshire, brick 1690; **Tushingham Church**, Cheshire, Gothic 1689-91; **Wilmslow**, Cheshire, Congregational Chapel, 1693.

Midlands – St Philip **Birmingham,** Archer 1710-15, St Modwen **Burton-on-Trent,** Staffordshire, W. & F. Smith 1719-26; St Saviour, **Foremark,** Derbyshire, Gothic 1662; **Ingestre Church**, Staffordshire, Wren 1673-6; SS. Peter & Paul, **Langton-by-Partney,** Lincolnshire, brick 1720-30; Holy Trinity, **Minsterley,** Shropshire, classical 1689;

St Philip's Cathedral, Birmingham, built in Baroque style by Thomas Archer in 1710-15.

St Mary the Virgin, **Monnington-on-Wye,** Hereford & Worcester-shire, 1679-80; St Mary, **Newent,** Gloucestershire, 1675-9; St Nicholas, **Nottingham,** brick 1671-82; St Mary, **Tyberton,** Hereford & Worcester, brick 1720; St Mary, **Warwick,** W. & F. Smith 1697; St Alkmund, **Whitchurch,** Shropshire, J. Barker 1712.

East – **Bury-St-Edmunds**, Suffolk, Unitarian Chapel, brick 1711-12; **Cambridge**: Emmanuel College Chapel, Wren 1668-74; Pembroke College Chapel, Wren (att.) 1663-5; St Catherine's College Chapel, Rbt. Grumbold 1674-86; **Ipswich**, Suffolk, Unitarian Meeting House, Jos. Clarke 1699-1700; All Saints, **North Runcton,** Norfolk, H. Bell (att.) 1703-13.

South – All Saints, **Bristol,** Avon, 1712-c.1716; St George, **Deal,** Kent, Sam. Simmons 1706, roof altered by J. James 1711-12; **Oxford**, Trinity College Chapel, B. Peisley 1691-4; St Catherine, **Wolverton,** Hampshire, brick recasing of older church 1717.

Scotland – **Alloa Church**, Central Region, Thos. Bachop 1680; **Lauder Church**, Borders Region, Wm. Bruce 1673; **Logie Church**, Fife Region, Thos. Bachop, Gothic 1684; **Tulliallan**, Fife Region, 1675.

Wales – St Mary, **Dolgellau,** Gwynedd, 1716; St Mary, **Cardigan,** Dyfed, 1702-3.

PALACES AND HOUSES

The 'Wren' style in country houses evolved naturally from the trend set by Sir Roger Pratt, the builder of Coleshill, Berkshire (1650s, burnt down 1952), and in the four other houses he built. The most influential of them was Clarendon House, Piccadilly, built in 1664-7 and demolished nearly twenty years later. His own house, Ryston

Hall, Norfolk (not open to the public) built *c.*1670 but altered in the 1780s and Kingston Lacy (NT), Dorset (1663-5 and altered in the 1830s) remain. Belton House (NT), Lincolnshire (1684-6), built by William Stanton but clearly influenced by Pratt reminds us of his importance. The 'Wren' style remained popular for some seventy years and is best seen in the quality clergy houses of cathedral closes, e.g. Mompesson House (NT), at Salisbury, Wiltshire, built in the first decade of the new century.

Belton House, Lincolnshire, built in 1684-6 by William Stanten in the style begun by Pratt at Coleshill.

In Scotland the 1707 Act of Union with England ended the possibility of wars, and building for defence was no longer a necessity. Sir William Bruce (1639-1710), the Scottish Surveyor-General, was responsible for Holyroodhouse, Edinburgh and Hopetoun as well as some fifteen other buildings. Drumlanrig Castle, Dumfries and Galloway, was built in 1675-89 for the 1st Duke of Queensberry by James Smith to designs attributed to Robert Mylne and is in a magnificent Scottish Baroque style. The building is a curious mixture of the Scottish castle tradition, with turrets at the four corners, and the classical style. The centre of the main front is dropped one storey to conform with the proportion of the applied Corinthian order decorating the façade. Fyvie Castle, built in 1600-3, makes no concession to the classical style on the exterior. It is the most French of the Scottish buildings of its time. The first three storeys are quite plain and restrained until the roof, where corbelled turrets with conical roofs, dormers and ornament break out in French Renaissance abandon.

Typical Features of Baroque Houses
The large houses are typified by their vast scale, curves, rounded arches and much exterior decoration with vases, figures, and military trophies.
Plan: Based on rectangles, the smaller houses consisting of a single rectangle and others, such as Belton, being three arranged in an H-form.
Elevation: The early buildings have little decoration on the exterior, often of brick with stone trim, two storeys plus attic, hipped roofs and dormer windows. The main entrance, up a short flight of steps, is the focal point of its façade. The doorway may be pilastered or have a heavy moulded surround, and few are without some form of portico or pediment, the latter triangular, segmental, broken or scrolled. Fanlights above the door light the hall or lobby. The door has four or six raised panels or, for the first time, glass panes in the upper half. The window tax, introduced in 1696 and only repealed in

Mompesson House, Salisbury, c.1701. The style begun at Coleshill was adapted to the comfortable houses of cathedral closes and exported to the Virginian colony.

1851, is responsible for some blocked windows but many were always so, introduced for symmetry. In larger houses there is a balustraded roof-walk and cupola. As the Baroque fashion progresses, giant orders decorate the elevations and parapet balustrades have vases and classical statues contributing to an exciting

Drumlanrig Castle, Dumfries and Galloway, built 1675-89 in a magnificent Scottish Baroque style for the first Duke of Queensberry.

Fyvie Castle, Grampian Region, is the most French of all Scottish castles of its time 1600-3. The oldest parts date from the thirteenth century.

CLASSICAL PEDIMENTS

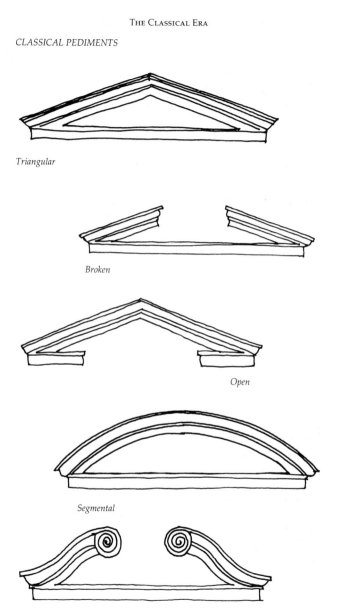

Triangular

Broken

Open

Segmental

Scrolled.

skyline. A pediment over the centre bays often marks the main entrance. Sliding sash windows were introduced from Holland in the 1680s; the originals have heavy glazing bars. Decorative ironwork for gates and railings, particularly in town houses.

Interior: Panelling with big rectangles and raised (bolection) moulding. Fireplaces of simple design with panels above for a mirror or painting. Panelled shutters act as primitive double-glazing. Impressive staircases, longer flights to accommodate higher rooms on the ground floors, landings, and heavy handrails supported by turned balusters. In smaller houses the balusters are often cut in silhouette because the joiner had no lathe. Bedrooms often on the ground floor. The grander houses have apartments for important visitors, with ceiling paintings of classical subjects reflecting the purpose of the different rooms and often expressing a compliment to the noble visitor. Aurora is a common bedroom ceiling subject and Apollo can signify William III. There is always a focal point marking the position of the important visitor. Lesser houses have plaster ceilings heavily decorated with swags of fruit and flowers.

Some Architects of the Period

Nicholas Hawksmoor (1661-1736): Employed as Wren's clerk in 1679, he soon became his valued assistant and colleague. Hawksmoor was Clerk of the Works at Kensington Palace and for the King William and Queen Anne blocks in the building of Greenwich Hospital. His first commission was for building Easton Neston (not open to the public), Northamptonshire, in 1695 for Lord Leominster.

Squerries Court, Kent, c.1680. A pediment over the centre bays often distinguishes the main entrance.

Thereafter he was involved with Vanbrugh at Castle Howard and Blenheim Palace as well as designing ten London churches following the New Churches Act of 1711.

Sir Roger Pratt (1620-84): Apart from making a six-year tour of Europe in 1664 Pratt was an untrained architect who had a remarkable influence. Coleshill (*c*.1650), Berkshire, which he built *c*.1652 (burnt down in 1952), for Sir George Pratt, in a simplified classical style, became the prototype for moderately large houses until the neo-Palladian phase of 1720. With Wren he was one of three commissioners appointed to supervise the rebuilding of the City after the Fire of 1666.

Sir John Vanbrugh (1664-1726): Jonathan Swift wrote that Vanbrugh 'without thought or lecture . . . hugely turn'd to architecture'. He made designs for Castle Howard, Yorkshire, in 1699 and the building began the following year with the assistance of Nicholas Hawksmoor. Before this, Vanbrugh had been successively a solder, prisoner in France and a playwright (when he built himself a theatre in the Haymarket). He succeeded William Talman as Comptroller of His Majesty's Works in 1702 and became Wren's principal colleague. Vanbrugh represents the ultimate in English Baroque; both Castle Howard (1700-26) and Blenheim Palace, Oxfordshire, of 1705-16 and completed by Hawksmoor in 1722-5 are vast conceptions of Baroque grandeur.

Sir Christopher Wren (1632-1723): The most famous of all British architects, if only because of his St Paul's Cathedral, London. He became Professor of Astronomy, Oxford, in 1661 and had no training at all in architecture. Owing only to his expertise in geometry and structures the King asked him to supervise fortifications at Tangier. He declined the request. His first commissions were for Pembroke College chapel (1663-5), Cambridge (att. to Wren), through the influence of his uncle the Bishop of Ely, and the Sheldonian Theatre (1664-9), Oxford. Wren made his only trip abroad, to Paris, in 1665. A year after the Great Fire of London in 1666, Wren was appointed Surveyor-General and principal architect for rebuilding the City, and in 1669 he was appointed to the post of Surveyor-General of the King's Works. Thereafter Wren's life was devoted to architecture and he evolved his distinctive classical version of the Baroque.

Where to See Examples

London – *College of Arms*, brick with stone trim 1671-88, Queen Victoria Street, EC4; *Fenton House* (NT), brick 1693, Hampstead, NW3; *Greenwich*: Hospital, Wren 1696 onwards; Royal Observatory, Wren 1675-6, Greenwich, SE10; *Hampton Court Palace* (HRP), Wren and Talman 1689-1702; *Ham House* (NT), brick with stone trim, modernised 1674, Richmond; *Kensington Palace* (RHP), brick 1661, Kensington, W8.

North – *Beningborough Hall* (NT), North Yorkshire, brick with stone trim, William Thornton 1716; *Beverley,* Municipal Offices, Humberside, The Hall *c*.1700; *Castle Howard* (Hon. Simon

Howard), North Yorkshire, Vanbrugh 1700-26; *Morpeth* Town Hall, Northumberland, Vanbrugh 1714; *Newby Hall* (Mr R.E.J. Compton), North Yorkshire, brick with stone trim 1690s; *Seaton Delaval* (Ld. Hastings), Northumberland, Vanbrugh 1720-28; *Wilberforce House* (Hull C.C.), Hull, Humberside, brick town house *c*.1660; *Yarm* Town Hall, Cleveland, brick 1710.

Midlands – *Ashdown House* (NT), Oxfordshire, rendered brick with stone trim *c*.1660; *Belton House* (NT), Lincolnshire, Wm. Winde (att.) 1685-88; *Blenheim Palace* (D of Marlborough), Oxfordshire, Vanbrugh & Hawksmoor 1707-25; *Boughton House* (D of Buccleuch & Queensberry), Northamptonshire, 1680s; *Chatsworth* (Chatsworth Ho. Trust), Derbyshire, Talman & Archer 1687-1707; *Ragley Hall* (M. of Hertford), Warwickshire, R. Hooke 1679-83; *Stanford Hall* (Ly. Bray), Leicestershire, W. Smith 1690s; *Tamworth,* Town Hall, Staffordshire, stone and brick 1701; *Worcester,* Town Hall, Hereford & Worcester, Thos White (att.) 1718.

East – *Cambridge*: St Catherine's College, Principal Court, Rbt. Gumbold, 1674-87; St John's College, Third Court, 1669-71; Trinity College Library, Wren 1676-84; *Felbrigg Hall* (NT), Norfolk, flint and brick enlarged 1674-87; *Great Yarmouth* Customs House, Norfolk, brick with stone trim 1720; *Kimbolton Castle* (Kimbolton School), Cambridgeshire, Vanbrugh 1707-10; *Kings Lynn,* Customs House, Norfolk, H. Bell 1683; *Wimpole Hall* (NT), Cambridgeshire, brick with stone trim, Gibbs 1690 & 1721.

South -*Abingdon,* Town Hall, Oxfordshire, C. Kempster 1678-80; *Anthony House* (NT), Cornwall, Gibbs & Moyle 1720-24; *Aynsham,* Town Hall, Oxfordshire, small late C17; *Dover,* Public Library, **Dover, Kent, Maison Dieu House 1665;** *Faringdon,* Town Hall, Oxfordshire, late C17; *Milton Manor* (Mrs Mockler), nr Abingdon, Oxfordshire, brick with stone trim 1663; *Oxford*: All Souls' College, North Ouad., Hawksmoor 1716-35; Brasenose College Library, J. Jackson (att.) 1656; Peckwater Quad., H. Aldrich 1704-14; Tom Tower, Wren 1681; Corpus Christi College, Wm. Townsend 1706-12; Old Ashmolean Museum, Thos. Wood 1678-83; Oriel College, Robinson Buildings, Wm. Townsend 1719-20; Queen's College, Front Quad., Wm. Townsend 1710-21; Sheldonian Theatre, Wren 1664-9; University College, Radcliffe Quad., 1717-19; Williamson Building, 1671-4; Worcester College, Hall and Library, Dr Geo. Clarke 1720. *Petworth* (NT), West Sussex, 1680s; *Squerryes Court* (Mr J. St A. Ward), Kent, brick 1680s; *Uppark* (NT), West Sussex, brick with stone trim, Talman *c*.1690 (recently damaged by fire); *Winslow Hall* (Sir E. Tomkins), Buckinghamshire, brick with stone trim, Wren (att.) 1698-1702; *Wooton Bassett,* Town Hall, Wiltshire, timber-framed upper floor 1700.

South-West – *Brympton d'Evercy* (Mr Clive-Ponsonby-Fane), Somerset, *c*.1670-80; *Dyrham Park* (NT), Avon, Talman & Hauduroy 1692-1705; *Kingston Lacy* (NT), Dorset, Pratt 1663-5; *Mompesson House* (NT), Salisbury 1701.

Scotland – *Brodie Castle* (NTS), Grampian Region, *c*.1610; *Drum-*

lanrig Castle (D. of Buccleuch & Queensberry), Dumfries & Galloway, early Scottish Baroque 1675-90; **Dumfries,** Town Hall, Dumfries & Galloway Thos. Bachup 1705; **Holyroodhouse Palace** (H.M. the Queen), Lothian Region, Rbt. Mylne and Wm. Bruce 1671; **Hopetoun House** (Hopetoun Ho. Pres. Trust), Lothian Region, Wm. Bruce 1699-1703, Wm. Adam 1723; **Lennoxlove** (D of Hamilton), Lothian Region, Wm. Bruce 1673-4 & 1676-7.

Wales – **Erddig** (NT), Clwyd, brick by Thos Webb 1684-7, wings 1723; **Monmouth,** Town Hall, Gwent, 1724; **Tredegar House** (Newport BC), Gwent, brick with stone trim 1664-74.

GARDENS

William III brought to England the idea of the smaller 'Dutch' water gardens. Westbury Court, Gloucestershire, has one that was laid out in 1696-1705. Like so much else, the influence on garden design came from the French Court and Versailles. Huge landscapes were created with rides ending in a focal point, or eyecatcher, cut through carefully planted woodland and straight canal-ponds terminating in fountains reflecting the passing clouds. Like the buildings decorated with urns and vases, the gardens also had vases, urns and classical creatures concluding some bosky ride. Again, the principle was that man's will had to be imposed on Nature. It was very labour intensive. Chatsworth, like many Baroque courtier-houses, was surrounded by a vast layout designed by the royal gardeners London and Wise. It was nearly all swept away by 'Capability' Brown in the mid eighteenth century. One such landscape survives at Bramham Park, Yorkshire. Of others, only remnants survive to remind us of the grandiose ideals of the Baroque period.

Where to See Examples

England – **Bramham Park** (Mr G. Lane Fox), West Yorkshire, *c*.1700; **Ebberston Hall** (Mr W. de Wend Fenton), remains of a larger garden laid out in 1718; **Hampton Court Palace** (HRP), London, remnants of a landscape laid out in the 1690s to complement Wren's additions in emulation of Versailles; **Kensington Palace Gardens** (HRP), London, W8., remnants of a scheme devised for William III in the 1690s. **Levens Hall** (Mr. C.H. Bagot), Kendal, Cumbria, topiary garden laid out 1692; **Melbourne Hall** (Ld Ralph Kerr), Derbyshire, remains of a much larger garden designed by London and Wise in *c*.1700; **Westbury Court** (NT), Gloucestershire, Dutch style watergarden laid out 1693-1704.

The Enlightenment

THE GEORGIANS 1720-1830

At the turn of the eighteenth century the ruling Tory party was in severe decline. They were associated with the Roman Catholicism of James II who was superseded by William III in the bloodless revolution of 1688, which they supported, also they had consorted with the Jacobite rebels. Their political deterioration caused a public rejection of the Tories who, after the Hanoverian succession in 1714, were excluded from office until the reign of George III. The fall of the Tories brought in the alternative political power, the Whigs, who were demanding many changes. The defeat of the French armies by the Duke of Marlborough caused a detestation of things French and Baroque. In any event, the great architects of the Baroque were either dead or very old and the style died with them. Prosperity was another factor. Between 1720 and 1770 exports doubled and the population increased from an estimated six millions in 1700 to an estimated nine in 1800. Landowners were increasingly prosperous and keen to replace their old-fashioned Tudor and Jacobean manors with something new. Moreover, the eighteenth century saw the peak of the popularity of the Grand Tour, the conclusion of a wealthy young man's education. Future patrons of architecture visited Roman sites in France and Italy and were well aware of what 'correct' architecture was about. This was the 'Age of Enlightenment'. Inigo Jones and, above all, Andrea Palladio became almost the only sources of true architectural enlightenment, until they were eclipsed in the 1760s.

The most influential of the future patrons of architecture to make the Grand Tour was Lord Burlington (1694-1753) who visited the Veneto in 1715 without, it seems, being impressed by Palladio's buildings. It was only after his return to England that the young Earl became interested in architecture, a love that never left him for the rest of his life. Through Burlington's powerful Court influence the course of Palladianism was set until the 1760s when a reaction against the straight-jacket imposed by the style moved architecture in other directions.

Palladianism was a British fashion. In France, the taste was for the Rococo, the last phase of European Baroque. The Rococo was a decorative style, light in character, contrasting with the heaviness of the Baroque. Asymmetrical and abstract and with sensuous C- and S-scrolls, the style was essentially French. The name is derived from the French word *rocaille*, meaning the shell and rockwork used in decorating grottoes. The Rococo had a small following in Britain as a reaction against the rigorous rules of Palladianism. An early example of English Rococo is the saloon at Ditchley Park, Oxfordshire, by James Gibbs with Rococo plasterwork of 1724 by the Italian Artari brothers, Vassali and Serena, the best craftsmen of their day. The supreme example is the interior of Claydon House in Buckinghamshire of 1757-69. English Rococo is distinguished by the playful use of mainly Chinese, Indian and Gothic forms. It was never a serious taste; rather, it was treated as a light-hearted decorative style applied to mirrors, furniture, picture-frames and overmantels and particularly to silver and gold plate, textiles and china. Architecturally, the style was used in garden buildings and grottoes where it all began.

In Scotland, William Adam (1689-1748), father of the better known Robert and James Adam, built up a wide and successful practice as a Palladian architect. His additions to Hopetoun House from 1723 made it the largest private house in Scotland. Floors Castle (1721-6)), Mellerstain (1725-6) and Duff House (1735-9) are only a few of the well-known buildings he altered or built.

The Rococo style was the last phase of Baroque and was purely decorative. Claydon House, Buckinghamshire, decorated inside by Luke Lightfoot in 1757-69 is in the Chinese style of which this doorcase is an example.

A Rococo garden monument to Congreve by William Kent 1736, at Stowe, Bucking-hamshire, where there is an extensive garden by Kent.

The rigid rules of Palladianism inevitably brought about its end. In 1758 Robert Adam (1728-92) returned from a four-year tour devoted to the study of Roman architecture in Italy. An object of his particular interest was the Palace of the Emperor Diocletian at Spalatro in what was then Dalmatia and a Venetian possession but is now Split in Yugoslavia. He had also visited Pompeii and Herculaneum and consequently was aware of Roman domestic architecture and interiors.

Within a few months of his arrival in London early in 1758 Adam secured commissions. He sensed the demand for change and gauged it correctly. Within a very short time Adam was busy with commissions. He offered the Neo-classical style based on his recent studies; it was not the old monumental architecture of Palladianism but an architecture based on genuine Roman domestic sources. Above all, it was new. The reaction of Sir Nathaniel Curzon, an early client in 1760, was typical of many of Adam's patrons. On seeing his proposals for rebuilding Kedleston Hall, Derbyshire, Curzon confessed himself to be 'struck all of a heap with wonder and amaze'. He had already employed two architects on the project, Matthew Brettingham and James Paine, both Palladians, and saw no reason why he should not have another change. Adam was initially employed to create a landscape around the half-built house. The Kedleston parkland that might be mistaken for 'Capability' Brown's, is possibly Adam's only landscape.

Adam employed 'movement' in his architecture; it was a return to the old Baroque feature of advancing and receding planes in contrast to the flatness of the Palladian façades. It is perhaps best seen on the south front of Kedleston Hall of 1760-70. From 1760-80 Adam was the most fashionable architect in Britain. When eventually patrons began to tire of his novelties, they turned to the more solid comforts of scholarship and precedent found in the work of Sir William Chambers, the most respected architect of his time.

The south front of Kedleston Hall, Derbyshire. The three centre bays (1760) by Adam give 'movement' to an otherwise flat Palladian facade.

Chambers was another Scot; but he was born in Sweden, trained in Paris, studied in Italy, travelled in the Far East and practised in London from his return to England in 1755. The oriental garden buildings at Kew (1757-63) are his; Chambers was the only British architect who had actually seen a Chinese building. Somerset

The Pagoda (1757-63), Kew Gardens, London, by Sir William Chambers. Chinoiserie was attempted by many but Chambers was the only architect to visit the Far East.

House, London (1776-96), designed for government offices, is his most worthy edifice, though lacking excitement. Its façade is that of a nobleman's country house set in the Strand. A classically correct Corinthian order through two stories is carried over a rusticated ground floor.

Inevitably, fashion turned against Neo-classicism and before the end of the century interest in it was waning. The fashionable client was faced with two alternatives: Greek or Gothic Revival. At the time the taste for Gothic was increasing, but the higher fashion was the Greek Revival. Greek architecture was inaccessible for all but the most intrepid of the grand tourists, since Greece was part of the Turkish Empire until 1829. However, James Stuart (1713-88), a Scottish architect, set out in 1751 in the company of a painter friend on a hazardous and exciting visit lasting three years. On their return they used the advertisement favoured by architects of the era and published drawings and illustrations of Greek remains under a long-winded title abbreviated to *Antiquities of Athens*. Thereafter Stuart was known as 'Athenian' Stuart because of his championing of the Greek Revival, although many were still uncertain which came first, the Romans or the Greeks. The Grecian fashion only really began in the 1780s. The simplicity and gravity of this early architecture were admired throughout Europe and the style reached the peak of its popularity in England in the 1820s and 1830s. Sir John Soane was the most successful proponent of the Greek style and is best known for his own house, Nos 13-14 Lincoln's Inn Fields, London (1812-34), now the Soane Museum. The Greek Revival had a far greater popularity in Scotland; Edinburgh was known as the 'Athens of the North' for its Greek Revival architecture.

The alternative Gothic Revival was a style that could be produced by every architect. It could also be used to modernize a house without going to the cost of rebuilding. Churches were often built in the Gothic style because it was felt to be a more appropriate style for churches. But, for domestic architecture, the style had never really vanished. We have seen the earlier revival of the style at Bolsover Castle in 1612, and both Wren and Kent contributed buildings in the Gothic taste; but this was not architectural fashion so much as clients' preference. For art history purposes, the Gothic Revival began in the mid eighteenth century and was inspired in the first place by amateurs and not professional architects. Horace Walpole (1719-97) remodelled his own house, Strawberry Hill, Twickenham, in the 'Gothick' taste, beginning in 1748 and using as his architect William Robinson. In no way were the Gothic principles of construction used; the remodelling only involved putting pretty plaster confections on a house already there. Many had a hand in the project, including Adam in 1766-7; it was only concluded by Walpole's death. Others, too, were infected by the Gothic fever and Sanderson Miller (1716-80), a gentleman architect, Gothicized the exterior and the hall of Lacock Abbey, Wiltshire, in 1753-5. A sham castle at Wimpole Hall, Cambridgeshire, is another of Miller's designs. He began

Somerset House (1776-96), London, and Sir William Chambers' best building. The Strand facade is in the Corinthian order over a rusticated ground floor.

his Gothic speciality by building a cottage on his Warwickshire estate, Radway Grange, in 1744, until fits of insanity in 1758 made more commissions impossible.

The most astonishing Gothic project was Fonthill Abbey in Wiltshire, built by James Wyatt in 1795-1812 for the sugar plantation millionaire, William Beckford, who, it was said, wanted to exceed in height the spire of Salisbury's cathedral. He achieved that ambition;

133

Sir John Soane's Museum, 13-14 Lincoln's Inn Fields, London, and originally Soane's own house, was built 1812-34 in the Greek Revival style.

Strawberry Hill, Twickenham, London. Horace Walpole's Gothic Revival house built 1749-76 by a 'Committee of Taste' that included Robert Adam. Walpole began the eighteenth century Gothic Revival.

Laycock Abbey, Wiltshire. Originally an Augustinian convent and enlarged in the 1750s by Sanderson Miller in the 'Gothick' style.

in true Gothic fashion the tower collapsed in 1825, but only after Beckford had to sell up owing to financial straights. The collapse was entirely owing to James Wyatt who never found time to supervise the commission. Most of what was left was subsequently demolished and only a low wing survives. Gothic remained a fashion from the 1750s, sometimes high-fashion, but then receded before returning to favour again. With a sketchy idea of history contemporaries were convinced that Gothic was the only truly English style.

GEORGIAN TOWNS

The best town planning was conceived in the eighteenth century. The London squares, beginning with Cavendish Square in 1717 and followed by Grosvenor Square (1720), Berkeley Square (1739) and ultimately Adam's Fitzroy Square in 1790, all developed by wealthy private landlords, gave elegance and peace to the outskirts of a busy capital city. Bath, the almost exclusive preserve of the architects John Wood (1704-54), and his son, another John (1728-81), began in 1729 with Queen's Square and culminated in the magnificence of the Royal Crescent. Completed in 1775, the crescent was invented by the younger Wood and was the forerunner of others in London, Edinburgh, Bath, Brighton, Bristol, Glasgow, Hastings, Leicester, Liverpool, Wisbech and Worthing. Elsewhere, further town schemes were undertaken with equally splendid results. Edinburgh New Town, planned by James Craig (1744-95) in 1763, was built by other architects; Robert Adam was completing Charlotte Square when he died in 1792 and William Henry Playfair continued where Adam stopped and built the very large Royal Terrace in the 1820s. Buxton in Derbyshire has a crescent by John Carr of York, built for the 5th Duke of Devonshire in 1780-90. The Paragon, Blackheath, Greenwich, S.E.3., by Michael Searles is one of the most elegant examples of urban planning anywhere. Manchester, Leeds, Liverpool and Bristol have remnants of past Georgian and Regency splendour, and many market towns owe their elegance to the classical detail of the surrounding eighteenth- and early nineteenth-century architecture.

The Royal Crescent, Bath, completed 1775 by John Wood, was the first crescent, and copied many times in other towns throughout Britain.

Number 6, Charlotte Square, Edinburgh, by Robert Adam who died in 1792 before it was completed.

CHURCHES AND CHAPELS

When a landowner had finished spending a fortune on rebuilding his house, he invariably had an attack of Christian conscience and built or rebuilt a church. The clients of Robert Adam were not immune from the feeling. After the 6th Earl of Coventry had Croome Court, Hereford & Worcester, built by Lancelot Brown in 1751-2 with interiors by Robert Adam, he turned their talents to the parish church, St Mary's, built in 1758-63 in Gothic Revival style complete with Rococo pulpit. Gunton Hall, Norfolk, built by Matthew Brettingham after 1742 in the Palladian style for Sir William Harbord, was followed by Adam's small St Andrew's church with its Neo-classical interior. Two church interiors of this period are outstanding: St Bartholomew's, Binley, West Midlands, a Neo-classical church built in the Adam style in 1773, was fitted out inside by Lord Craven as a saloon 'in the ballroom taste', while St John's, Shobdon, Hereford & Worcestershire, has an interior in the best Rococo Gothic style furnished with huge white-painted box pews, a three-decker pulpit and two Gothic chairs, all by the Hon. Richard Bateman of Shobdon Court, who was a friend of Walpole's.

Of the Neo-classical architects, Adam built very few churches, Chambers and Holland effectively none at all. A number of minor churches were built in this period, notably All Saints', Newcastle-on-Tyne, of 1786 by David Stephenson, with an elliptical nave and St Chad's, Shrewsbury, of 1790 by George Steuart with a circular nave. Both derive from a preliminary design by Gibbs for St Martin-in-the-Fields, London. John Carr built the church at his birthplace, Horbury, Yorkshire, at his own expense in 1791-3 in a Neo-classical style, aisleless with a tunnel-vaulted nave, on an octagonal plan. At Paddington Green, W.2, St Mary's is a late Palladian gem by John Plaw (c.1745-1820), built in 1791 using the 14in. Venetian foot, and recently restored.

The wars of 1793-1815 slowed down building activities but not the influx of populations to the manufacturing towns. Consequently there was a shortage of churches in the newly developed urban areas. To correct this ecclesiastical imbalance, the Church Commissioners' Act for the building of economical preaching boxes was passed in 1818. In fact, none of the new churches cost more than £18,000 and economy was the keynote.

Smirke, Soane and Nash, the three Crown architects of the Office of Works designed some of the new churches but the need for large economical churches defeated even Soane's ingenuity. St Peter's Walworth (1823-4), Holy Trinity, Marylebone Road (1826-7), and St John's, Bethnal Green, (1826-8) are all Neo-classical and not among his best works. Nash's All Souls', Langham Place (1822-5) is the only survivor of three Commissioners' churches in Regent Street. Outside London, one of Soane's pupils, George Basevi (1794-1845), best known for his Fitzwilliam Museum, Cambridge (1836-45), was more successful with St Thomas's, Stockport (1822-5), entered from the east end through a portico.

Preceding the New Churches Act by two years and costing £70,000 was St Pancras New Church designed by W. and H.W. Inwood in the Greek Revival style whose portico on Euston Road is a reproduction of the Erectheion, Athens. Scotland adopted the Greek Revival for most of the churches of the early nineteenth century. St Giles's, Elgin, by A. Simpson and of 1827-8, is the most impressive of the Greek Revival churches in Scotland.

Gothic and Nonconformist church architecture of this period is less impressive. Both denominations opted in the main for Greek Revival. The Catholic churches at Walsall (1825-7) and Wolverhampton (1827-8) by Joseph Ireland (1780-1841) are both Grecian, yet by the

1830s Catholics had turned to the Gothic Revival; they were doing no more than following fashion.

LANDSCAPES AND GARDENS

In the parks of the great houses change had overtaken the old labour-intensive Baroque gardens. It is open to question who began the move with the 'natural' Rococo gardens; but Horace Walpole, who usually had something apposite to say, claimed that William Kent 'Leaped the fence and saw that all Nature was a Garden . . . ' Certainly, in the 1740s at Rousham Park in Oxfordshire, Kent's best known landscape, there are winding paths with glimpses of distant statues and temples. The curves and bends of the walks are in the best Rococo tradition and quite unlike the strict geometrical design of the earlier vast Baroque landscapes. Another Rococo garden of the 1740s survives at Painswick House in Gloucestershire, but it is not so complete as that at Rousham. These early natural gardens were comparatively small in scale and were in their turn swept away by the huge landscapes of Lancelot, 'Capability', Brown (1716-83).

Brown began his professional life as a gardener and in 1741 at Stowe, Buckinghamshire, worked as Kent's assistant. His landscapes were encircled by a belt of trees and the park itself was laid out with clumps of trees – his critics called it 'clumping and belting'. The clumps were brilliantly contrived so that, as one rode up the drive, the views constantly changed; the best view of all, that of the approaching house, was teasingly kept back until the last minute. Flower beds around the house did not exist, meadow grass came up to the windows and ha-has kept deer and grazing animals away. Any flower gardens were banished behind the walls of the distant kitchen garden. Later, Brown engaged in architecture, with some thirty-four buildings to his credit. Although most of them are garden buildings, he was responsible for some substantial commissions; but his extensions at Corsham Court, Wiltshire, in 1761-4 and Claremont House, Surrey, 1771-4, built in collaboration with H. Holland, are his only larger buildings open to the public.

While 'Capability' Brown had done away with flower gardens near the house, an opposing force in the next generation of gardeners sought to bring them back. Humphrey Repton (1752-1818), realizing that his wealthy clients had parks that had to be 'naturally' planted, continued the Brown tradition away from the main house. But around the house itself Repton devised 'artificial' gardens in contrast to the open natural parkland. The flower beds were often circular, the grass was mown and smooth and there were conservatories and gravelled walks. There were also cottages, garden houses and bridges. Repton brought a picturesque informality to the proximity of the house, a garden style that continued into the 1830s long after the fashion for 'clumping and belting' had passed.

Where to see Examples

Painshill Park (Painshill Pk. Trust), Surrey 1738-73; **Painswick** (Ld.

Dickinson), Gloucestershire, remarkable garden of 1740s; Rousham (Mr Cotterell-Dormer), Oxfordshire, William Kent 1740s; **Stourhead** (NT), Wiltshire, 'Claudian' garden laid out 1741-80.

THE PALLADIAN PHASE 1720-60

Palladianism covered four decades when the designs of Palladio and his followers were considered the only 'correct' classical style. Unlike the Baroque, which was a way of life, Palladianism was purely architectural and intellectual. The classical orders are used correctly and, while the façades are relatively flat with an attached or project-

Holkham Hall, Norfolk. One of the grandest Palladian houses of England, built 1731-56 for the first Earl of Leicester by William Kent, Matthew Brettingham and Lord Burlington.

ing portico, the interiors are contrastingly rich. The great Whig palaces such as Holkham and Houghton, both in Norfolk, were built with impressive rooms of entertainment expressing the old passions of power and wealth for political ends. Some of these rooms would be used by the family in their everyday life; Holkham's dining room on the *piano nobile* was used by the Cokes but the state bedchamber on the same level was kept exclusively for important visitors.

The names of Palladian architects are too many to list; however it is noteworthy that a high percentage originated in Scotland and came to England to build up a successful practice.

Some Architects of the Period

Colen Campbell (1673-1729): A Scot, he sensed the need for change in the early eighteenth century. He was a lawyer turned architect and first published his three-volume *Vitruvius Britannicus* in 1715, 1717 and 1725. The book, consisting of plates of modern British architecture, was self-advertisement with a message. The message was the superiority of 'Antique Simplicity' (classical Roman) over the 'affected and licentious' forms of the Baroque. The 'renowned Palladio' and the 'famous Inigo Jones' were both recommended as the only architects of merit.

Henry Flitcroft (1697-1769): A joiner by training, he was a protégé of Lord Burlington and consequently a convinced Palladian. His rebuilding and enlarging of Wentworth Woodhouse (*c.*1735-70), Yorkshire, unfortunately only occasionally open to the public, is his largest and best known commission. More accessible is his work at

Wimpole Hall, Cambridgeshire (refronted and altered in 1741-5).

James Gibbs (1682-1754): Was born near Aberdeen and studied architecture in Rome. Best known for his Cambridge Senate House (1722-30) and the Radcliffe Camera, Oxford (1737-48), he was responsible for either building, remodelling or adding to some fifty private houses, including Anthony House (1720-4), Cornwall, and Ditchley Park (1720-31), Oxfordshire. He gave his name to the 'Gibbs surround'.

Useful Dates

1715-60: Palladianism. Began with Colen Campbell's Wanstead House, Essex (now demolished), in 1715 and based on the ideals, principles and plans of Andrea Palladio (1508-80).

1724-60: Rococo. A reaction against Palladianism.

1760-90: Neo-classicism. Created from Robert Adam's studies of Roman domestic architecture.

1750s to 1870: Gothic Revival.

1780s to 1840s: Greek Revival. A continuation of Neo-classicism.

The Radcliffe Camera, Oxford, built 1737-48 by James Gibbs. A Baroque building with a dome after St Peter's, Rome.

Where to See Examples

London – **Chiswick House** (DOE), designed for himself by Lord Burlington in 1723 and based on the Villa Capra, Vicenza; **Marble Hill** (EH), Roger Morris 1724-9, Twickenham; **Strawberry Hill** (Theological College), Horace Walpole and others 1748-97, Twickenham (open by application to the Principal).

North – **Abbot Hall** (Lake Dist. Mus. Trust), Kendal, Cumbria, John Carr 1759; **Beverley,** Guildhall, Humberside, remodelled by William Miller 1762-5; **Dunham Massey** (NT), Cheshire, remodelling of an older house by John Norris 1732-40, east wing altered by John Shaw

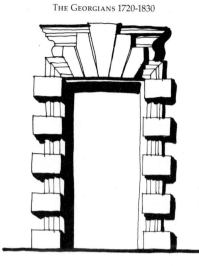

Doorway with 'Gibbs Surround', an early Palladian feature.

1822; **Hovingham Hall** (Sir M. Worsley), North Yorkshire, rebuilt by Thomas Worsley 1750s; **Lyme Park** (NT), Cheshire, remodelling of an older house by Giacomo Leoni 1725-35; **Nostell Priory** (NT), West Yorkshire, James Paine *c*.1737-*c*.1750, interior by Robert Adam 1765-75; **Ormesby Hall** (NT), Cleveland, middle-sized country house *c*.1750 with original interiors; **Rokeby Park**, County Durham, Thomas Robinson *c*. 1735; **Sledmere House** (Sir T. Sykes), Humberside, *c*.1751.

Midlands – **Chillington Hall** (Mr P. Gifford), Staffordshire, F. Smith 1725-9, remodelled by John Soane 1785-9; **Ditchley Park** (Ditchley Fdn.), Oxfordshire, F. Smith to designs by James Gibbs 1720-30; **Hagley Hall** (Vct. Cobham), West Midlands, Sanderson Miller 1754-60; **Mawley Hall** (Galliers Trustees), Shropshire, F. Smith 1730; **Woburn Abbey** (D. of Bedford & Bedford Ests.), Bedfordshire, rebuilt by Henry Flitcroft 1747-61; **Rousham Park** (Mr C. Cottrell-Dormer), Oxfordshire, wings, north front and garden buildings by William Kent 1738-41.

East – **Euston Hall** (D. of Grafton), Suffolk, remodelled by Matthew Brettingham 1750-6; **Holkham Hall** (E. of Leicester), Norfolk, William Kent and Matthew Brettingham 1731-56; **Houghton** (M. of Cholmondeley), Norfolk, Colen Campbell 1722-35, interior by William Kent.

South – **Broadlands** (Ld. Romsey), Hampshire, remodelled by L. Brown 1766-8; **Clandon Park** (NT), Surrey, Giacomo Leoni *c*.1730-3; **Lacock Abbey** (NT), Wiltshire, Gothic interior and exteriors by Sanderson Miller 1754-5; **Stourhead** (NT), Wiltshire, Colen Campbell 1720-4, wings added 1793-5.

South-West – **Hatch Court** (Com. Barry Nation), Somerset, Thomas Prowse 1761; **Trewithin** (Mr A.M.J. Galsworthy), Cornwall, Thos Edwards *c*.1738-40.

Scotland – **Duff House** (NTS), Grampian Region, William Adam 1735-9; **Floors Castle** (D. of Roxburgh), Borders Region, William Adam 1721-6, remodelled by W.H. Playfair 1837-45; **Glasgow**, Pollok House (City of Glasgow D.C.), Strathclyde Region, 1747-52 additions by Rowland Anderson 1890-1908; **Hopetoun House** (Hopetoun Ho. Preservation Trust), Lothian Region, enlarged and remodelled by William Adam 1723-48; **Mellerstain** (E of Haddington), Borders Region, wings by William Adam 1725-6.

THE NEO-CLASSICAL PHASE 1760-90

It was Robert Adam's genius to recognize the need for change and to offer clients exactly the new architecture for which they were looking. His work can never be described as other than exciting and this is how his patrons saw the result. We have already seen at Kedleston how he livened up exteriors by 'movement'. His south front at Kedleston is based on the genuine Roman precedent of the Arch of Constantine and the Saloon behind it with its deeply coffered dome, on the Pantheon. Adam went even further into Roman originals for the interior; for not only was the entrance hall based on Vitruvius's Egyptian Hall but it also represented the first courtyard of a Roman villa or palace, the atrium. This hall was not open to the sky as a Roman atrium would have been, but was ceiled over and lit by two occuli, or round skylights. The saloon off the hall represented the Roman living room, or *vestibulum*. This intellectual exercise was carried even further. The rooms to the east of the hall were rooms of taste and intellect devoted to music and literature (the library) while those to the west catered for the physical demands of food and sleep (the dining room and the state bedchamber).

Adam's buildings always contain much more than is perceived at first glance. At Syon House, Middlesex, a remodelling in 1762-9 of an older building, the soft tones of the admittedly very grand marble entrance hall do nothing to prepare one for the astonishing gold architecture of the south ante-room that follows. Neither is one prepared for the contrast of the very long, narrow library into which one next passes. In all his interiors Adam's work is distinguished by the decorative use of 'grotesques'. These are fanciful decorations in paint or plaster resembling the arabesques used by the Romans on walls of buildings that, when discovered, were underground and believed to be 'grottoes' (from which comes the name). At his death in 1792, Adam was building the University, Edinburgh, eventually completed by Playfair in 1817-26.

A chimney board at Osterley Park, London, designed by Robert Adam in the 1770s using 'Grotesques' based on original Roman decoration found in ruins below ground and thought to be grottoes.

Some Architects of the Period

John Carr (1723-1807): A mason with no architectural training, Carr nevertheless built up a busy practice in Yorkshire and the north of England. The exterior of Harewood House, Yorkshire (1759-71 altered by Barry 1843-50), is his but the interior is wholly Adam's. The Town Hall and Assembly Rooms, Newark, Nottinghamshire (1773-6) and the Assembly Rooms, Buxton, Derbyshire (1780-90) are two examples of his public buildings. His exteriors are severely plain, reflecting the Neo-classical principles of logical construction and truth to materials.

George Dance junior (1741-1825): Like Adam, Dance was the son of an architect, and he visited Italy in the same year as Adam returned. Soon after Dance returned in 1764 he designed the remarkable All Hallows' church, London Wall (1765-7). The fine detail of the interior of the church owes something to Adam's style and is a notable performance for a young man of twenty-four. In 1768 Dance became one of the founder members of the Royal Academy. Unfortunately, his best buildings, Newgate Prison (1770-80) and the Council Chamber, Guildhall, London (1777-8), have been demolished, but the façade of his Theatre Royal, Bath (1804-5) remains.

Henry Holland (1745-1806): Worked as assistant to Lancelot Brown and married his daughter. Holland's style was a simplified Adam manner with a French influence. His most famous commission was for the future Regent's Carlton House, London (1783-95 but demolished), where he employed French assistants. Dover House, Whitehall, S.W.1., built by James Paine in 1754-8, was remodelled by Holland in 1787 giving Whitehall its finest architecture excepting Jones's Banqueting House. At Berrington Hall, Herefordshire (1778-81), Holland created an interior with spacial effects anticipating Soane's work.

Harewood House, West Yorkshire. The work of two architects; John Carr for the Palladian exterior and Robert Adam for the neo-Classical interior, built 1759-71.

James Wyatt (1746-1813): The son of an architect, Wyatt was born into a prolific and confusing family of architects. He took the almost compulsory study tour of Italy where he trained in Venice and Rome, returning to England about 1768. He was a brilliant but facile designer who could turn his hand to anything from a close imitation of Adam interiors to the Greek Revival style – and still make a speciality of the Gothic Revival. He enjoyed a huge practice; but the majority of his commissions were for additions and interiors, for example his alterations and stable yard at Ragley Hall, Warwickshire, in 1779-97. Wyatt can never be forgiven for his disastrous restoration of Salisbury Cathedral that included destruction and alterations 1789-92.

All Hallows, London Wall. Built 1765-7 by George Dance Junior when he was twenty-four. The design detail is in the Adam neo-Classical style introduced in 1760.

Sir John Soane (1753-1837). He was assistant to Henry Holland and he later, like so many of his contemporaries, studied architecture in Italy. His individual interpretation of classical architecture and eccentric style is instantly recognizable. His exteriors exhibit a restrained linear decoration and occasional dramatic skylines introducing bases and sacophagi, as at, for example Dulwich Art Gallery, South London built 1811-14. Soane's interiors are equally dramatic in their use of intersecting arcs and domes.

Dulwich Picture Gallery, London. The first nineteenth century public picture gallery built 1811-4 by Sir John Soane in his dramatic abstraction of the Classical style.

Where to See Examples

London – *All Hallows*, George Dance 1765-7, London Wall, EC2; *Apsley House* (Trusts. of V & A Mus.), Robert Adam 1778-8, enlarged and refaced by B. & P. Wyatt 1828-9, Hyde Park Corner, SW1; *Kenwood House* (EH), remodelled by Robert Adam 1767-9, Hampstead Lane, NW3; *Osterley Park* (Trusts. of V & A Mus.), remodelled by Robert & James Adam 1763-80, Isleworth; *Syon House* (D. of Northumberland) remodelled by Robert Adam 1762-9, Brentford.

North – *Harewood House* (E. of Harewood), West Yorkshire, John Carr 1759-71, Robert & James Adam interiors 1759-71, altered by Charles Barry 1843-50; *Heaton Hall* (Manchester Art Galleries), Lancashire, rebuilt by James Wyatt *c.* 1772; *Newby Hall* (Mr. R.E.J. Compton), North Yorkshire, remodelled by Robert Adam *c.*1770-*c.*1780; *Richmond*, North Yorkshire, Theatre Royal, the country's oldest theatre *c.*1788; *Stockeld Park* (Mr. P.G.F. Grant), North Yorkshire, James Paine 1758; *Cannon Hall* (Barnsley MBC), South York-

148

shire, John Carr 1764-8; **Tatton Park (NT),** Cheshire, Samuel Wyatt 1784-91 completed by L.W. Wyatt 1807-13; **York**, North Yorkshire, Fairfax House (York Civic Trust), town house by John Carr *c*.1765.
Midlands – **Althorp** (E. Spencer), Northamptonshire, remodelled by Henry Holland 1787-9; **Attingham Park** (NT), Shropshire, George Steuart 1783-5; **Berrington Hall**(NT), Hereford & Worcester, Henry Holland 1778-81; **Buscott Park** (NT), Oxfordshire, 1780; **Kedleston Hall** (NT), Derbyshire, transitional Palladian by Matthew Brettingham *c*.1758, James Paine 1759-60 with south front and interior by Robert Adam 1760-70, park also by Adam; **Luton Hoo** (The Werner Family), Bedfordshire, exterior by Robert Adam 1767, interior C20; **Shobdon**, Hereford & Worcester, St John's Rococo-Gothic fantasy by the Hon. Richard Bateman 1752-6; **Shugborough Hall** (NT), Staffordshire, remodelled by Samuel Wyatt 1790-80.
East – **Wimpole Hall**(NT), Cambridgeshire, remodelling of an older house by Henry Flitcroft 1742-5, library interior by James Gibbs 1719-21, Gothic tower by Sanderson Miller 1749-51.
South – **Asgill House** (Asgill Ho. Trust), Surrey, Robert Taylor 1760-5; **Basildon Park** (NT), Berkshire, John Carr 1776, interiors J. Papworth 1839-44; **Belmont Park** (Harris (Belmont) Charity), Kent, Samuel Wyatt 1787-92; **Claremont** (Claremont Fan Court Fdn.), Surrey, L. Brown 1771-4; **Claydon House** (NT), Buckinghamshire, an older house added to 1757-71 with Rococo interiors by Luke Lightfoot, enlarged by Thomas Robinson 1768-77; **Corsham Court** (Ld. Methuen), Wiltshire, enlarged by L. Brown 1761-4; **Goodwood House** (D. of Richmond), West Sussex, enlarged by James Wyatt 1787 onwards; **Hatchlands Park** (NT), Surrey, Robert Adam interiors 1758-61; **Stowe House** (Stowe School & NT), Buckinghamshire, south front by Robert Adam 1771, remarkable landscape by Vanbrugh, Bridgeman, Kent and Brown; **Gorhambury** (E. of Verulam), Hertfordshire, Robert Taylor 1777-90.
South- West – **Bath**, Avon, No. 1 The Royal Crescent (Bath Pres. Trust), John Wood the Younger 1767-75; **A la Ronde** (NT), Devonshire, large sixteen-sided 'cottage orné' with shellwork interiors 1795; **Saltram House** (NT), Devonshire, remodelled interior by Robert Adam 1768-9; **Ugbrooke House** (Ld. Clifford), Devonshire, rebuilt in castle style by Robert Adam 1763-71.
Scotland – **Culzean House** (NTS), Lothian Region, castle style by Robert Adam 1777-92; **Edinburgh**, Lothian Region, The Georgian House (NTS), Robert Adam 1791, Charlotte Square; **Gosford House** (Ld. Wemyss Trust), Lothian Region, Robert Adam 1790-*c*.1800, wings demolished *c*.1810, rebuilt 1883-91 by W. Toung; **Mellerstain** Borders Region, castle style by Robert Adam 1770-80.

THE REGENCY 1811-30

The time span is very arbitrary; but George IV, who was king from 1820 to 1830 and Regent from 1811 to 1820 during his father's insanity, was a man of an original taste that he indulged extravagantly. His influence during this short period cannot be overlooked. We have briefly mentioned the oriental flavour introduced at Kew by William Chambers in his garden buildings of 1757-63. These were merely two eye-catchers and it was not until 1803 that the first 'Indian' building went up. This was Sezincote, Gloucestershire, built by S.P. Cockerell (1754-1827) for his brother, a retired East India nabob.

Sezincote was only first by a short head. At Brighton in 1804 the future king had William Porden (1755-1822) build domed stables (now Concert Hall) for his Pavilion. Humphrey Repton, who had advised at Sezincote, was called in to redesign the old Pavilion and the Regent was 'enchanted'. After that nothing happened until John Nash (1752-1835) took over in 1815. The Regent's oriental fantasy reached its conclusion in the form we know it today in 1821.

The Greek Revival increased in popularity during this period eventually to be superseded by the Gothic Revival in the 1830s. The rigid adherence to classical rules was abandoned and some very interesting buildings were put up. Reference has been made to the Wyatt family of architects and to James Wyatt; his nephew. Jeffry Wyatt (1766-1840), did much restoration and remodelling of Windsor Castle for George IV and William IV in 1824-40, for which he was knighted. He had already changed his name to Wyatville, a wise move to avoid confusion with the other fourteen architects produced by the Wyatt dynasty. Wyatville worked on some seventy buildings mainly in the 'castle' style and with very mixed results. His remodelling of Wollaton Hall, Nottingham, from 1803 to 1825 when he destroyed almost all the original interiors can only be regretted, yet his completion of, and additions to, the Gothic Ashridge Park in 1814-21 must surely be applauded.

The 'Picturesque' style of the Regency period should not be overlooked. Originally, the term 'picturesque' was applied to the eighteenth-century landscapes created in imitation of the paintings of imaginary classical landscapes of the Roman Campagna by such

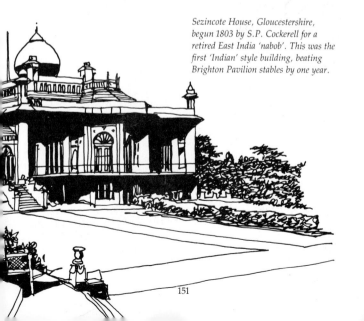

Sezincote House, Gloucestershire, begun 1803 by S.P. Cockerell for a retired East India 'nabob'. This was the first 'Indian' style building, beating Brighton Pavilion stables by one year.

The Royal Pavilion, Brighton. The Prince Regent's Eastern fantasy by John Nash and built 1815-21. The stables, built 1804, are now the Concert Hall.

seventeenth-century painters as Poussin and Claude. By the Regency period the term was applied to the 'cottage orné', a deliberately contrived rustic cottage or gate lodge, and to the Italianate and castellated country houses of John Nash, of the type, say, of Nash's own Blaise Hamlet in Gloucestershire, begun in 1810. Blaise was a model 'picturesque' village which became the prototype for others, such as Old Warden in Bedfordshire (1830s), Edensor on the Chatsworth estate, Derbyshire (1838-42) and Somerleyton, Suffolk (1850s). However, Nash's Blaise Hamlet was not the first of the picturesque villages; if the façades dated in the 1790s are correct then Harlaxton village in Lincolnshire precedes Blaise Hamlet. But its cottages were built by the landowner George de Ligne Gregory and later re-modelled; some have half-timbered additions, others are in Tudor style, some are vaguely classical and most have a well-head in the front garden.

John Nash was the last of the town planners of vision. His stuccoed Regency terrace houses of the 1820s in Regent's Park, London, brought classical grace to the area, but they were only part of a great processional way which he planned from Buckingham Palace to Regent's Park by way of Carlton House. The plan was never achieved owing to the death of George IV in 1830, but Buckingham Palace was turned essentially into its present form by Nash in 1825-30 before William IV appointed Edward Blore to succeed him.

Outside London, the Greek and classical styles were used for town developments with elegant brilliance. Cheltenham owes much of its grace to J.B. Papworth (1775-1847) who completed schemes in the 1820s and 1830s; Decimus Burton (1800-81) designed the Calverley estate in Tunbridge Wells, Kent, at the same period and at Newcastle-on-Tyne, Tyne and Wear, John Dobson (1787-1865) was doing similar work in the 1830s.

In Scotland, the 'picturesque' took on a peculiarly Scottish flavour. Sir Walter Scott, the celebrated historical novelist, carried his romanticism into the building of Abbotsford in 1816, extended in 1822-3. Abbotsford is in the Scottish baronial style evoking a romantic past that never was, and with it Scott created the Scottish Baronial style of the nineteenth century.

Ashridge Park, Hertfordshire. A sympathetic Gothicizing carried out by James Wyatt 1808-13 and completed by Jeffrey Wyatville in 1814-21.

Where to See Examples

London – ***Dulwich Art Gallery***, John Soane 1811-14, Dulwich. SE21; ***Pitshanger Manor*** (London B. of Ealing), John Soane 1800-4, Ealing, W5; ***Sir John Soane's Museum***, John Soane 1812-13, Lincoln's Inn Fields, WC2; ***Theatre Royal***, Benjamin Nash 1811-12, Drury Lane, WC2.

North – ***Belsay Castle*** (EH), Northumberland, Greek Revival begun 1807 by Charles Monck.

Midlands – ***Belvoir Castle*** (D. of Rutland), Gothic remodelling by James Wyatt 1801-13, Leicestershire, serious fire 1816, restored by Rev. J. Thoroton; ***Eastnor Castle*** (Mr J. Hervey-Bathurst), Hereford & Worcester, castle style by Robert Smirke 1812-20; ***Hardwicke Court*** (Mr C.G.M. Lloyd-Baker), Gloucestershire, Robert Smirke 1817-19).

East – ***Ickworth House*** (NT), Suffolk, Francis Sandys 1796-1803 and c.1825-30.

South – ***Ashridge Park*** (Gvnrs. Ashridge Man. Coll.), Hertfordshire, Gothic style by James Wyatt 1808-13 completed by Jeffry Wyatville; ***Brighton***, East Sussex, Royal Pavilion, John Nash 1815-22; ***Knebworth House*** (Ld. Cobbold), Hertfordshire, rebuilt in Tudor Gothic style by John Redgrave 1813, reconstructed by H.E. Kendall 1844; ***Dinton House*** (NT), Wiltshire, Jeffry Wyatville 1814-7; ***Sezincote*** (Mr D. Peake), Gloucestershire, the first 'Indian' style house by S.P. Cockerell 1805, oriental water-garden by Repton and Daniell.

Blaise Hamlet, Gloucestershire. A 'picturesque' cottage in the village by John Nash from 1810.

Abbotsford, Borders Region. Built 1816-23 by William Atkinson for Sir Walter Scott in a romantic Gothick style that began the Scottish Baronial style.

South-West – ***Arlington Court*** (NT), Devonshire, Thomas Lee 1720-3; ***Claverton Manor*** (American Mus. in Britain), nr Bath, Avon, Jeffry Wyatville *c*.1820 but interior is North American.

Scotland – ***Abbotsford*** (Mrs P. Maxwell-Scott), Borders Region, Walter Scott's romantic vision of the Gothic style by William Atkinson 1816-23; ***Dalmeny House*** (E. of Rosebery), Lothian Region, Tudor Gothic by William Wilkins 1814-17; ***Glasgow***, Strathclyde Region, Hutcheson Hall (NTS), David Hamilton 1802-5.

Wales – ***Gwrych Castle*** (Miss J. Donald), Clwyd, designed by the owner, L.B. Hesketh and others in the 'picturesque' castle style, completed 1815; ***Penrhyn Castle*** (NT), Caernarvonshire, rebuilt in 'Norman' style by Thomas Hopper *c*.1825-1844.

THE VICTORIAN ERA

The Battle of the Styles and after: 1830-1900

The 'battle' was simply that of 'foreign' classical styles against English Christian Gothic. Gothic gained steadily through the century until the 1870s when its popularity waned. A sample of Victorian country houses shows the trend: in 1840-4 41 per cent. were built in the classical style, in 1850-4 32 per cent., in 1860-4 only 16 per cent. The plainness of the classical style did not attract the Victorians; they had money to spend and associated plainness with meanness. The alternative to plainness was richness and to them that meant decoration. Up to the 1860s the decoration was mainly Gothic, but there were exceptions.

By the 1840s the most popular architectural styles were Greek Revival, evolving into Rococo Revival, while Romanesque, Tudor and Elizabethan, Italianate and English Decorated Gothic were all patronized. In the following decade, Greek and Romanesque had all but vanished and French, Italian and German Gothic mixed with Renaissance motifs had taken over, with a heavy version of French Renaissance. This lasted until the 1870s. By the end of the 1860s a correct English Gothic was introduced and the Arts and Crafts movement began. Derived from that movement was the 'Queen Anne' style of the 1870s. It was really nothing to do with Queen Anne; the vogue incorporated many historical styles and descended through the social ladder to public house architecture by the 1890s. The 1890s saw a revival of the old Baroque and even the Adam Neoclassical style. The underlying current beneath all this stylistic confusion is that early Victorian architecture was marked by an enthusiasm for historicism. From the 1850s to 1870s there was a revolt from historicism with a preference for coarse, strong shapes, developing into a late Victorian taste for more delicate, fussy ornament and a marked movement away from Gothic.

In October 1834 the old Houses of Parliament were burnt down. Immediately a debate began about the rebuilding and in 1835 a competition was held to find the best design. It is significant that the style was required to be either Gothic or Elizabethan: it was felt that these were the only architectural styles that were genuinely English. Sir Charles Barry won the competition. It was a peculiar choice. He was known for his buildings in the Italianate style, his Travellers' Club (1829), for instance, in Pall Mall, London; but, when the new Houses of Parliament were completed in 1870, Barry was dead and the applied Gothic decoration was looking distinctly old-fashioned.

The Gothic detail of the Houses of Parliament was supplied by Augustus Welby Pugin, using Gothic sources for his designs. Pugin approached Gothic architecture with a religious fervour and recommended Gothic as the only 'true' architecture. His preference was for fourteenth-century English Decorated, yet he used Perpendicular Gothic for the Houses of Parliament.

This enthusiasm for 'true' Gothic was also shared by John Ruskin (1819-1900), a theorist and not an architect, who had enormous influence on architecture after the publication of his *Seven Lamps of Architecture* in 1849. He recommended Sacrifice (architecture, as against mere building, must take account of the beautiful), Truth (no disguised strengthening, no pretence materials and handwork rather than machine work) and Life (the study of natural forms). Stucco and plaster masquerading as stone and houses pretending to be castles were out. The University Museum, Oxford (1855-60, by Thomas Deane and Benjamin Woodward) was closely supervised by Ruskin and incorporated many of his Gothic ideals. The brilliant use of cast-iron, which lends itself to Gothic construction, is a curious choice when Ruskin hated the metal. Clearly the Picturesque was dead. This message was taken up by William Morris in the 1860s.

Like Ruskin, Morris was no architect but a practical man of enormous energy who in his own words 'wanted to change the world'. His was a reaction against the poor design of machine-made goods. From Morris's recommendation that the craftsman should also design, as had the medieval craftsman, came the Arts and Crafts movement. This in its turn influenced architects such as C.F.A. Voysey (1857-1941), C.R. Mackintosh (1868-1928), the American architect Frank Lloyd Wright (1869-1959), and the international architect Walter Gropius (1883-1969).

In Scotland, the Baronial style set by Abbotsford became almost universal for country houses. Queen Victoria bought the Balmoral estate near Ballater in 1848. On it already was a modest house built by John Smith of Aberdeen in the 1830s. In 1853-5 Prince Albert employed Smith's son, William, to enlarge the building in the Scottish Baronial mode with towers, turrets and castellations that immediately became the fashion for all Scotland.

The Early Years 1830-50

As with everything they did, the Victorians entered the battle with enthusiasm. It was no good just rejecting classical architecture; there had to be a reason. According to Pugin, classical architecture was foreign and pagan, whereas Gothic was English and Christian. While the classical style might be acceptable in towns and cities, it should never be seen in the English countryside. Pugin went on to demonstrate that the plan of a building came before appearance. This resulted in symmetry being thrown away and asymmetrical façades becoming fashionable.

Not everyone, however, was persuaded that Pugin had got his facts right; many took the Elizabethan style to be more suited to England. All were agreed that there must be no fudging the truth of construction and materials. Ashlar stone replaced cement render (which might be right for the dry Mediterranean but was impractical for damp Britain). There were exceptions to stating the truth; in the early days of plumbing tanks were required to be placed high up to

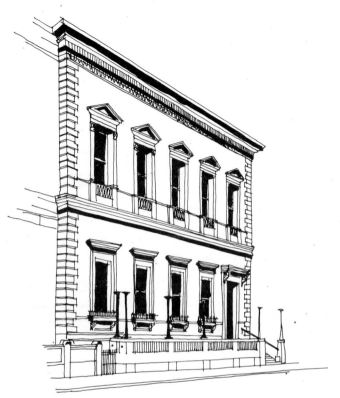

Travellers' Club, Pall Mall, London, by Sir Charles Barry. The facade, rendered in stucco, is that of an Italian Palazzo.

give pressure, and the skylines of Victorian houses are dotted with towers of all kinds disguising water tanks!

The Italianate style was considered acceptable for clubs and the sea coast. Osborne House, Cowes, Isle of Wight, with its two towers, one for observation and the other for holding a water tank, was begun in 1845 and might have been designed for the Italian Riviera. It was designed by Thomas Cubitt and overseen by Prince Albert. Cubitt was an able property developer rather than an architect, and much of Bloomsbury, almost all of Belgravia and parts of Pimlico are due to him. It is to be regretted that the Victorian Royal family never engaged an architect of genius, particularly as Prince Albert was personally concerned about the quality of design and art.

The period 1830-50 was a time of innovation. Cast-iron, pioneered in industrial buildings, was used as a fire-proof material and brick vaulting supported on cast-iron girders is concealed above the ceilings of many Victorian country houses. Sir Joseph Paxton (1801-65), built the Crystal Palace for the Great Exhibition of 1851 using iron and glass, then an amazing innovation. Gas lighting had been used at Dundonald Abbey in Scotland in 1787 and by Walter Scott at Abbotsford in 1823. It was unpopular because it was smelly and the light was unflattering, faults unresolved until the gas mantle was invented in 1887. The heat and smell from gas lighting resulted in high rooms to take away the offensive odours.

In the cities and towns where ever larger factories demanded ever larger work forces in times of prosperity (and ruthless sackings in the frequent slumps) the population increased in unrestrained poverty. Christian architecture did not imply Christian charity to one's countrymen.

The Greek Revival continued into the 1830s, represented by the now demolished Euston Arch, London (1836-9), by Philip Hardwick, Dundee High School (1832-4) Tayside Region, by G. Angos, and C.R. Cockerell's Ashmolean Museum, Oxford (1839-45), all examples of the contemporary notion that the style was more suitable for a town environment.

Some Architects of the Period

Sir Charles Barry (1795-1860): A leading architect of the early Victorian period, whose work spans the Regency as well, Barry could turn out any style a client demanded. Highclere Castle, Hampshire (1842-50) is in the Elizabethan style, Cliveden, Buckinghamshire (1850-1) is in Italian Renaissance style (and unusually built of brick faced with Portland cement) while Halifax Town Hall (1859-62) is classical with a pagoda-like spire.

William H. Burn (1789-1870): A Scottish architect who built up the biggest architectural practice in Victorian Britain. He, like Playfair, trained with Smirke in his London office, which explains his skill with the Greek Revival style. Before deserting Edinburgh for London in 1844 to concentrate on his enormous private house practice, he designed St John's church, begun in 1816 and described as 'a free rendering of English Perpendicular', and the Melville Monument (1821-2), both in Edinburgh. Very different is his John Watson's Hospital at Belford, near Edinburgh, with large windows seeming almost modern. In England, Burn was known for his planning of complicated service wings with rooms for every speciality. Unfortunately, his early promise in Scotland did not last and his English country houses lack spirit.

William Henry Playfair (1789-1857): Although considered a Scottish architect, he was born in London. He moved to Edinburgh in 1804 and later trained with Smirke where he acquired a taste for the Greek Revival. Returning to Edinburgh he won the competition for the completion of Adam's University building in 1816. There are

Halifax Town Hall, West Yorkshire. Built 1859-62 by Sir Charles and E.M. Barry in a Venetian Renaissance style with a Pagoda-like spire. Cloth had made Halifax wealthy and the Town Hall expresses new wealth.

buildings by Playfair all over Edinburgh, but he is best known for his Royal Institution of 1822-6 (now the Royal Scottish Academy) and National Gallery of Scotland 1850-7.

Augustus Welby Pugin (1812-52): Although immensely influential on nineteenth-century architecture, he was not a prolific architect, mainly because from 1836 he was responsible for the Gothic detail interiors and furnishings of the New Palace of Westminster. His conversion to Catholicism also cut him off from many commissions. Nottingham Cathedral (1841-4), Scarisbrick Hall, Lancashire (1837-45), and Alton Towers, Staffordshire (1837-52) are only a few of his best buildings in the Gothic style. St James's (RC), Reading (1837-40) is one of his rare designs in the Romanesque. Pugin also built two cathedrals (RC), St Chad's, Birmingham in 1839-41, St Mary's, Newcastle-on-Tyne in 1841-44. All are, inevitably, in the Gothic style. From 1827-51 he published some fifteen books promoting the Gothic style for architecture as well as for furniture and jewellery.

Sir Robert Smirke (1780-1867): Worked briefly in Soane's office before travelling for four years in Germany, Italy and Greece. His foremost building, the British Museum (1823-47), shows his attachment to Greek Revival and the Ionic order. Eastnor Castle, Hereford & Worcester (1812-20), in symmetrical Gothic, and the conversion of Burlington House into the Royal Academy in the 1860s are two examples showing his versatility. He was a pioneer in the use of concrete foundations and cast-iron beams and rescued buildings in trouble such as Millbank Penitentiary and the Custom House.

The British Museum, London: Built 1823-47 by Sir Robert Smirke in the Greek Revival Ionic order. It remains his best building.

Alexander Thomson (1817-75): Many notable buildings in and around Glasgow by 'Greek' Thomson have been sadly neglected, vandalized or demolished. Of his three churches only the St Vincent Street church (1859) remains operational. Impressively built in a strict Greek classical style, it is neglected by the district council which owns it. His Egyptian Halls (1871-73) in Union Street, built as a warehouse, is a surprise and deserves a better fate than the street-level shop fronts with which it is disfigured. Local authorities have been criminally neglectful and continue to be so. Sadly many of his best tenements and warehouses were demolished in the 1960s. It is to be hoped that the recently founded Alexander Thomson Society can retrieve his reputation and what remains of his work.

Where to See Examples

London – *Linley Sambourne House* (Vic.Soc.), a town house of the 1840s, 18 Stafford Terrace, W8.
North – *Arley Hall* (Hon. M.L.W. Flower), Cheshire, in Jacobean style by J. Latham 1833-41; ***Scarisbrick Hall*** (Scarisbrick School), Lancashire, Gothic-Tudor style by A.W.N. Pugin 1837-45 and E.W. Pugin 1862-8; ***Peckforton Castle*** (Graybill Ltd), Cheshire, Salvin's recreation of an Edwardian castle 1844-52.
Midlands – *Alton Towers*, Staffordshire, Gothic alterations and additions by A.W.N. Pugin 1836 onwards, now a ruin; ***Flintham Hall*** (Mr M.T. Hildyard), Nottinghamshire, coarsely classical by T.C. Hine 1851-4; ***Knebworth*** (Ld Cobbold), Hertfordshire, Tudor house remodelled in Gothic style by H.E. Kendall 1842; ***Wrest Park*** (EH), Bedfordshire, French Rococo style by Earl de Grey 1834-6.
East – *Somerleyton Hall* (Ld. Somerleyton), Suffolk, vaguely Tudor by John Thomas 1844-52.
South – *Albury Park* (Co.Hos.Ass.), Surrey, Gothic-Tudor re-modelling by A.W.N. Pugin 1846-52; ***Highclere Castle*** (E. of Caernarvon), Hampshire, reconstructed in Elizabethan style by Barry 1838-44; ***Osborne House*** (EH), Isle of Wight, Italianate style by Thos Cubitt and Prince Albert 1844-8.
Wales – *Bodel Wyddan Castle* (Clwyd C.C.), Clwyd, Gothic re-modelling 1830-40 by Hansom & Welch.

THE HIGH VICTORIAN PHASE 1850-80

By mid-century Gothic was winning the battle. The fashion was a curious mixture of English Gothic with French, Venetian and Italian versions. Symmetry was deliberately avoided. Kelham Hall, Nottinghamshire (1859-64), by Sir George Gilbert Scott and now the headquarters of the Newark and Sherwood District Council, has no fewer than fourteen different types of Gothic windows on the west front alone. The result is not restful and nor did the house ever work properly. Yet it must have pleased Scott, because he repeated the Kelham formula at Preston Town Hall (1861-4 demolished) and at St Pancras Station Hotel, London, (1868-76). Alfred Waterhouse (1830-1905) did the same when he built Manchester Town Hall in 1869 and

repeated much of the same detail of Gothic turrets, clock tower and roofscape when he built Eaton Hall (now demolished), Cheshire, for the Duke of Westminster in 1870-82.

The problem for High Victorian design was how to reconcile strength with richness; the answer was to ornament construction and construct ornament. Muscularity was in and feebleness out. The delicate patterns, naturalistic ornament and soft tints of the 1840s gave way to the chunky, massive and masculine in the 1860s and 1870s. There was one fault with Gothic; it evolved as church architecture and not as a domestic style. There was a gradual realization of this fact and by the 1870s Gothic was becoming a style primarily for church building. The first high Victorian church was All Saints', Margaret Street, London W.1, by William Butterfield (1814-

Kelham Hall, Nottinghamshire, in asymmetrical High Victorian Gothic by Sir George Gilbert Scott in 1858-61. The interior was never completed – the builder ran out of money.

1900), begun in 1849. All Saints' is severe and geometrical with an interior covered in coloured marbles and polychromatic brick patterns – a very far cry from the rural English parish church pattern of a few years earlier.

In London, the last of the great square-building phases was developed in Onslow Square in the 1860s with terraces of very large Italianate houses. The building of Grosvenor Bridge and Victoria Station in 1862 brought development in Fulham and West Kensington of identical streets of identical two-storey terraced houses, many of which display token Gothic capitals on their front bay window. In 1863 the world's first underground railway opened from Paddington to Farringdon, a forerunner of other lines, permitting the extension of London beyond the radius of the horse-drawn omnibus.

Carlton Towers, North Yorkshire. The staircase tower is a good example of 'muscular' architecture. Built 1873-5 by E. W. Pugin in an uncompromising Gothick style.

All Saints', Margaret Street, London, the first high Victorian church, built 1849-59 by William Butterfield.

The creation of the far-reaching Arts and Crafts movement by William Morris in the 1860s, as a reaction against machine-made products, was initiated by the building of his first house, Red House, Bexleyheath, Kent (1859), by his friend and colleague Philip Webb. This was a welcome relief from the overheated designs of the metropolis and a reassertion of English Domestic values.

Some Architects of the Period

Anthony Salvin (1799-1881): A prolific and long-lived architect known for his country houses in the Tudor and Elizabethan style. A pupil of Nash, he had designed three large country houses by the time he was thirty, Mamhead, Devon (1828-38) in the Tudor style, Moreby Hall, Yorkshire (1828-33), also Tudor and Harlaxton Manor, Lincolnshire (1831-7), in the Elizabethan style. By the end of his life he had built, rebuilt, altered or extended some seventy-six country houses as well as restored the Tower of London and Windsor Castle.

Sir George Gilbert Scott (1811-78): The foremost practitioner and spokesman of the mid Victorian Gothic Revival. Scott became a casualty in the Battle of the Styles when, after nailing his flag to the Gothic masthead, Lord Palmerston forced him to design the new Home Office and Foreign Office, Whitehall (1868-73), in the Italia-

The Foreign Office, Whitehall, London. Built 1868-73 by Sir George Gilbert Scott. Lord Palmerston insisted on Italianate style and got it!

nate style. Scott was the leading architect for Victorian churches and was often criticized for his church restorations. Scott's St Mary's Episcopal Cathedral, Edinburgh, a late work consecrated in 1879, is his most successful recreation of thirteenth-century Gothic. Perhaps best known for St Pancras Station Hotel (1868-76) and the High Victorian Albert Memorial (1863-75), both in London.

St Mary's Cathedral, Edinburgh. A successful recreation of a pure thirteenth century Gothick style by Sir George Gilbert Scott in 1874-1917.

George Edmund Street (1824-81): Worked for a time in Scott's office before starting his own practice in 1849. William Morris, Philip Webb and Norman Shaw all trained under Street 'in the nursery of the Arts and Crafts'. As an ecclesiastical and domestic architect, Street was a strong exponent of the Gothic style. One of his most powerful churches is St John the Divine, Kennington (1870) but he is best known for the last major Gothic Revival building in London, the Law Courts, a commission he won in a competition set in 1866. It was strongly criticized at the time which is perhaps another way of saying it is good architecture.

William Burges (1827-81): A High Victorian apostle of English Gothic forms, he was also a great believer in plenty of carved decoration and consequently on the fringes of Morris's Arts and Crafts movement. His work is always distinctive and particularly so in the enlargements he made to Cardiff Castle (1865-85) and in his rebuilding of Castle Coch, near Cardiff (1872-9). The interiors of both are a riot of colour and carved decoration that is often amusing in its use of fiends, goggle-eyed frogs and monkeys. With such an idiosyncratic style he had no imitators.

Philip Speakman Webb (1831-1915): A great architect of the late Victorian Domestic Revival. He trained with Morris in Street's office and he and Morris became life-long friends. In 1859 Webb designed for Morris, Red House at Bexleyheath, Kent, a prototype for dis-

St Pancras Station Hotel and offices, London, in high Victorian Gothick Revival, including Venetian Gothick, by Sir George Gilbert Scott in 1868-76.

Red House, Bexleyheath. The first Arts and Crafts house, built for William Morris by his friend Philip Webb in 1859.

criminating middle-income clients, a new class of patron. Webb's houses were based on vernacular architectural styles. His last commission was Standen, near East Grinstead, Sussex (1891-4) in which local materials and the local vernacular style blend with simplicity and infinite care.

Where to See Examples

London – *Dulwich College*, Dulwich, SE21, newer buildings in Italianate Renaissance style by Charles Barry junior 1866-70; *Leighton House* (B. of Kensington & Chelsea), Holland Park Road, W14, town house by George Aitchison 1866; *Little Holland House* (B. of Sutton), Carshalton, Arts and Crafts town house built for himself by Frank Dickinson 1874; *Red House* (Mr Hollamby), Bexleyheath, the first Arts and Crafts house, built 1859 by Philip Webb for William Morris.

North – *Allerton Park* (G.A. Rolph Foundation), North Yorkshire, Gothic-Elizabethan by James Firth 1852; *Alnwick Castle* (D. of Northumberland), Northumberland, complete remodelling in Gothic castle style with Italian Renaissance interiors by Salvin 1852-61; *Bowes Museum*, County Durham, French Second Empire by Jules Pelechet 1870; *Carlton Towers* (D. of Norfolk), North Yorkshire, remodelling in Gothic-Tudor style by E.W.N. Pugin 1873-5 and J.F. Bentley 1875-7; *Cragside House* (NT), Northumberland, large rambling house by Norman Shaw 1869-84, first to be lit by electricity in 1880; *Holker Hall* (Mr H. Cavendish), Cumbria, part Elizabethan and part Gothic styles by Paley and Austin c.1873.

Midlands – *Harlaxton Manor* (University of Evansville), Lincolnshire, Elizabethan Baroque by A. Salvin 1831-7 and W. Burn 1838-54; *Oxford*, University Museum by B. Woodward 1855-60; Keble College by W. Butterfield 1873-6.

Standen, West Sussex, by Philip Webb in the Arts and Crafts Domestic Revival style.
Built 1891-4 as a holiday and weekend house for a successful London solicitor.

South – *Clivedon* (NT), Buckinghamshire, Italianate style by Barry 1850-1; *Hughendon Manor* (NT), Buckinghamshire, remodelled in Tudor style by E.B. Lamb 1862; *Waddesdon Manor* (NT), Buckinghamshire, French Renaissance style by G.H. Destailleur 1879-89.
South-West – *Dunster Castle* (NT), Somerset, extensive Gothic alterations by Salvin 1868-72; *Knightshayes Court* (NT), Devon, early-Gothic style by Wm Burges 1869-71.
Scotland – *Balmoral Castle* (H.M. the Queen), Grampian Region, Scottish baronial by William Smith 1853-5; *Torosay Castle* (Mr C. James), Strathclyde Region, Scottish baronial completed by David Bryce 1858.
Wales – *Bodrhyddan Hall* (Ld. Langford), Clwyd, large additions and remodelling of a C17 brick house by W.E. Nesfield 1872-4.

THE DOMESTIC REVIVAL 1880-1900

The battle of the styles ended inconclusively. Although Gothic made considerable gains against the classical style as the century progressed, the Gothic influence had all but vanished by 1900. This was mainly due to the Arts and Crafts movement led by William Morris. Architects such as Shaw and Eden Nesfield, who began their professional life dedicated to Pugin's Gothic principles, were soon pioneering domestic applications of the 'Queen Anne' and 'Old English' mansion styles decorated with sunflowers, both potted and unpotted, and friezes of Japanese disc ornaments called by both architects 'pies'. Bedford Park, Turnham Green, then well

'Pies' by W.E. Nesfield 1868 and a favourite Arts and Crafts motif. Sunflowers in a two-handled pot by W.E. Nesfield 1868, another Arts and Crafts favoured motif.

beyond the edges of built-up London and away from any commercial development, was laid out by Shaw in 1876 and consists of small, mainly semi-detached houses with 'Queen Anne' detailing.

Shaw was nothing if not versatile; to him must be credited the first 'skyscraper' construction in Britain. In using this steel-framed technique the weight of exterior walls is carried on steel cross-members at each floor level and not by the wall itself as with traditional construction methods. At No. 17 Chelsea Embankment (Old Swan House) of 1876, the finest 'Queen Anne' house in London, the weight of the upper floors is carried on a cantilever steel-frame.

Not all architects of the 1880s felt compelled to follow the 'Queen Anne' trend. Collingham Gardens, London S.W.5, by Ernest George and Harold Peto in 1881-7, is a square with various houses, all designed with gables in the Dutch fashion and nothing approaching the 'Queen Anne' style. In adjacent Harrington Gardens are two more examples of their work built in 1882, No. 19 for W.S. Gilbert and another for Sir Ernest Cassel, the banker. Both are examples of the George and Peto domestic style, again with no hint of the 'Queen Anne' style. Neither is there any suggestion of Gothic or classical styles.

Another Arts and Crafts architect, C.F.A. Voysey (1857-1941), set up in practice in 1882 and specialized in a traditional, low, big roofed, rural style. At No. 14 South Parade, Bedford Park, Voysey deliberately contrasted the surrounding pretty brick houses with the tall Studio House, an outstanding example of the Arts and Crafts covered in white roughcast render with stone trim.

Prototype design for two semi-detached houses planned for Bedford Park, London, by Norman Shaw and published in Building News *16th November 1877.*

Some Architects of the Period

Richard Norman Shaw (1831-1912): Trained under William Burn, where he began a life-long association with W.E. Nesfield, and shortly afterwards took Philip Webb's place in Street's office. Shaw, in private practice with Nesfield, evolved a new sophisticated range of domestic styles employing vernacular motifs that became the basis of much of the late Victorian Domestic Revival. Cragside, Northumberland (1869-84), is an early masterpiece in a mixture of styles but at Bedford Park Shaw compromised between 'Queen Anne' and 'Old English'. New Scotland Yard (1887-90 & 1906) is in a then fashionable Baroque Revival style.

William Eden Nesfield (1835-88): Trained briefly in Burn's office with Shaw and then with his uncle by marriage, Salvin. A brief period in Paris introduced him to French Gothic Revival. Nesfield

Swan House, Chelsea Embankment, London. Built by Norman Shaw in 1876 using steel-frame construction and the finest 'Queen Anne' domestic building in London

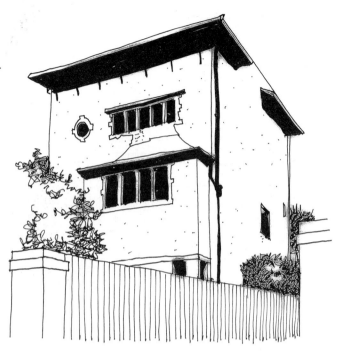

Studio House, Bedford Park, London. Built by Voysey 1889-94 and one of London's outstanding Arts and Crafts Houses. Voysey deliberately contrasted the neighbouring houses with a simple, tall style and rendered instead of the usual 'Queen Anne' brick.

shared an architectural practice with Shaw 1863-76. His small Wren Revival lodge (1866) in Kew Gardens is the first example of the 'Queen Anne' style. Kinmel Park, Clwyd (1868-71, and not open to the public) is in a 'Revived Classical' style and another pioneering 'Queen Anne' design.

William Morris (1834-96): Not an architect, although he trained briefly with his friend Webb in the Oxford office of G.E. Street. Street was a High Church architect who influenced Morris with Gothic detail. Morris was the leader of the Arts and Crafts movement and advocated a return to the medieval principles of craftsmen designing and designers being craftsmen. From this came the 'Queen Anne' style of architecture of the 1870s. Morris promoted the idea of the garden suburb, where the inhabitants had convenient access to the countryside and the beneficial effects it afforded. Ebenezer Howard followed him in 1898 when he published *Tomorrow*, outlining the rural ideal of the garden city that was eventually realized in Hampstead Garden Suburb, London N.W.11, begun 1906 and involving Lutyens, Baillie Scott, Parker & Unwin and others. Comprising freestanding, semi-detached and terraced houses, Hampstead Garden Suburb is built mainly in neo-Georgian and country vernacular styles.

Cragside, Northumberland, built from 1869 to 1874 for an armaments manufacturer, Lord Armstrong, by Norman Shaw in the Domestic Revival style of the Arts and Crafts movement.

Useful Dates
Greek Revival: Continued until the 1840s.
Gothic Revival: Continued until the 1870s. Delicate patterns in 1840s, 'muscularity' 1860s-70s.
Arts and Crafts movement: Began in the 1860s.
1870s to 1890s: 'Queen Anne' style.
1890s: Baroque and Adam Revivals.
1890s to 1910: 'Domestic' Revival.

Where to See Examples
England – *Cambridge*, Newnham College, Queen Anne style by B. Champneys 1892-3; *Lotherton Hall* (Leeds Metro D.C.), West Yorkshire, remodelled in Georgian style 1896 and 1903; *Standen* (NT), West Sussex, rural vernacular with Arts and Crafts interiors, by Philip Webb 1891-4; *Wightwick Manor* (NT), Staffordshire, half-timbered revival by Edward Ould 1887-93, Arts and Crafts interiors.

Scotland – *Glasgow*, Strathclyde Region, The Tenement House (NTS), a first floor flat in tenement built 1892.

VICTORIAN CHURCHES

In the more than sixty years of Queen Victoria's reign some 600 new churches were built by the Church of England to cater for the population of the rapidly expanding towns and cities. Other denominations built even more. The fashion in church building was overwhelmingly Gothic. In the early years, the style was Perpendicular, applied to what was basically a classical building. Under Pugin's influence, church design became structurally Gothic and by mid-century the preference was for fourteenth-century Decorated – the High Victorian style – and Ruskin's devotion to Venice promoted outbreaks of Venetian Gothic. Towards the end of the century, there was a marked return to Early English Gothic. The creation of new dioceses, a necessity in the face of increasing population, caused the building of the first Anglican cathedral since Wren's St Paul's, Truro's Gothic cathedral begun in 1880 by J.L. Pearson and only completed in 1947.

Lodge at Kew Gardens, Surrey. Built by W.E. Nesfield in 1866 and the first of the 'Queen Anne' Revival.

Besides this frenzy of building many more churches were enlarged and drastically restored. Unfeeling restoration by Sir George Gilbert Scott provoked William Morris into organizing public opinion against such insensitive work and forming the Society for the Preservation of Ancient Buildings (S.P.A.B.) in 1877. It was nicknamed the 'Anti-Scrape' society in reference to one hated method of restoration, the scraping of moss and lichen from bare stone surfaces.

Circumstances resulted in a demand for new Roman Catholic churches and buildings: the Catholic Emancipation Act of 1829 and, in France, the withdrawal of State support for the religious teaching orders, an influx of Irish Catholics and the expansion of towns. John Francis Bentley (1839-1902), a convert to Roman Catholicism, took many commissions in and around London; but his most important work is Westminster Cathedral striking in its Byzantine style and consecrated in 1910 after his death. The Byzantine choice was tactful because the building was not far from Westminster Abbey, which was thought to rule out Gothic, and the nearby Brompton Oratory in an Italian Baroque inhibited the use of that style. The final extraordinary choice offended no one.

Westminster Cathedral, London, in an unusually striking Byzantine style, so avoiding a clash of styles with Westminster Abbey and the Brompton Oratory. Built 1894-1903 by J.F. Bentley.

Some Church Architects of the Period

John Dando Sedding (1838-91): As a pupil of Street, Sedding might be expected to have been dedicated to Gothic but this was not so. He was, closely associated with the Arts and Crafts movement. His Holy Trinity church, Sloane Street, S.W.1., begun in 1888 in a free Gothic style, is known as a 'temple of the Arts and Crafts'. Unusually for the nineteenth century, his Holy Redeemer, Clerkenwell, E.C.1., begun in 1888, is in a free Italian Renaissance style.

George Frederick Bodley (1827-1907): The late Victorian counterpart of Pugin in his support for the late Gothic manner. Bodley was Scott's first pupil, but he favoured more simple decorative designs. He was an early supporter of the William Morris firm and St Martin's, the major architectural thrill of Scarborough, Yorkshire (1861-2), contains some of the firm's first work. Bodley's finest church is his miniature cathedral in Clumber Park, Nottinghamshire, begun in 1886 for the Duke of Newcastle.

Where to See Examples

Period 1830-50: *Bath*, St Michael, Gothic by G. Manners 1835-7; *Birmingham*, St Chad RC Cathedral, North German Gothic by Pugin 1839-41; *Cheltenham*, St Peter, neo-Norman by S.W. Daukes 1847-9; *Derby*, St Mary RC church, Perp. by Pugin 1839; *Edinburgh*, Tolbooth St John's church, Perp. by J.G. Graham 1842-4; *Leeds*, Mill Hill Unitarian chapel, Perp. by Bowman & Crowther 1847; St Saviour, Ellerby Rd., Gothic by J.M. Derick 1842-4; *London*, St Dunstan-in-the-West, Fleet St., by J. Shaw 1829-33; St Giles, Camberwell, SE5., Gothick by Sir George G. Scott 1841-3; St Thomas RC church, Rylston Rd., Fulham, SW6., by Pugin 1847; *Manchester*, St Luke, Cheatham Hill Rd., Perp by T.W. Atkinson 1836-9; *Nottingham*, St Barnabas RC Cathedral, Derby Rd., Early English by Pugin 1841-44.

Period 1850-80: *Babbacombe*, Devon, All Saints, polychrome by W. Butterfield 1865-74; *Doncaster*, South Yorkshire, St George, Sir George G. Scott 1854-8; *Edinburgh*, St Mary's Cathedral, Sir George G. Scott 1874-1917; *Glasgow*, St Vincent St. church, A. Thomson 1859-61; *London*, All Saints, Margaret St., W1., W. Butterfield 1850-9; St Augustine, Kilburn, NW6, J.L. Pearson 1870-80; St James-the-Less, Pimlico, SW1., G.E. Street 1860-1; St John the Divine, Kennington, SE11., G.E. Street 1870-89; St Mary Abbots, Kensington, W8;, C13 Gothic by Sir George G. Scott (1870-2); *Oxford*, Keble College chapel, W. Butterfield 1873-6; *Scarborough*, North Yorkshire, St Martin, G.F. Bodley 1861-2.

Period 1880-1900 *Clumber Park chapel*, Nottinghamshire, Bodley & Garner 1886-9; *London*, Holy Redeemer, Clerkenwell, EC1., J.D. Sedding 1888-90; Holy Trinity, Prince Consort Rd., SW7., Bodley & Garner 1900-8; *Holy Trinity*, Sloane St., SW1., J.D. Sedding 1888-90; *Westminster Cathedral*, SW1., J.F. Bentley 1894-1903; *Watford*, Hertfordshire, Holy Rood RC church, J.F. Bentley 1883-90.

NINETEENTH-CENTURY GARDENS

The most influential Victorian writer on gardens, John Claudius Loudon (1783-1843), had an influence on garden design still evident today in the laid out beds of municipal gardens. Loudon took the 'natural' garden of Repton and adapted the style to the smaller sub-urban and villa gardens, so introducing the 'gardenesque', an ugly word for an ugly style. He recommended that 'the hand of man should be visible in the natural style as in the most formal geometric style'. It was a formula for the 'display garden' and for a return to the old principle that nature must be controlled and it was a fashion that continued to the end of the century. Loudon also recommended the planting of foreign trees and shrubs and these, too, are with us today in the form of vast redwoods, ridiculous-looking Chilean pines or 'monkey puzzle' trees and other trees quite alien to Britain. Fashion in the 1840s was for the Italian Renaissance garden. Although Barry's great house itself has gone, the Italian garden at Trentham Park, Staffordshire (1834-40) with its balustrades and formal beds is still maintained. Osborne House (1844-8) on the Isle of Wight, built in the Italianate style, understandably has an Italian ter-raced garden with fountains and balustrades in elegant and charm-ing proportion.

The Elizabethan parterre garden enclosing hedges forming pat-terns was an historical revival brought in by W.E. Nesfield in the 1860s and, because he trained in the office of his uncle Anthony Sal-vin, the later Salvin houses often have Nesfield gardens. By the 1880s another change in fashion was launched by William Robinson (1838-1935), a return to the natural garden, which he called the 'wild' garden, in which roses climbed and creepers wandered. This suited many owners of large houses who were suffering a serious drop in rental income owing to the agricultural slump of those years: they could not afford the many gardeners needed to maintain the old-fashioned, labour-intensive layouts. This 'careless' style of garden led naturally to the even less intensive gardens of Gertrude Jekyll (1843-1932) that were ideal for the Domestic Revival house of the 1880 and 1890s. Indeed, it would be difficult even today to find a garden border not planted in her manner, in skillfully arranged groups of colours and shades.

Where to See Examples

Alton Towers, Staffordshire, Italian garden with a 100ft pagoda, created by the 15th Earl of Shrewsbury 1814-23, with additions by W.E. Nesfield in 1857; *Athelhampton* (Lady Cooke), 'Tudor' garden created by Inigo Thomas *c*.1900; *Chatsworth* (Chatsworth House Trust), Derbyshire, a huge garden added to what was left of another garden made in 1700, mainly obliterated by Capability Brown in 1760, vast rocks and cascades, an arboretum and pinetum with a conservation wall and a now vanished conservatory by the 6th Duke of Devonshire and Joseph Paxton from the 1830s; *London*, Crystal Palace, Sydenham, the formal Italian parterres are being restored to their original splendour, together with the educational 'prehistoric' lake, all by Joseph Paxton in the 1850s; *Biddulph Grange*, (NT) Staffordshire, a very individual garden created by James Bateman in the 1850s; *Scotney Castle* (NT), picturesque garden made round a castle ruin by Edward Hussey and W.S. Gilpin in 1830s.

INDUSTRIAL ARCHITECTURE

Initially, industry produced no architecture. The builders of the first spinning mills in the late eighteenth century made no Grand Tour and did not throw money away on unprofitable building frills, neither did they employ architects. Sir Richard Arkwright's Masson Mill on the Derwent near Matlock, Derbyshire, built in 1783, has a four-storeyed entrance with a cupola and Venetian windows this

Masson Mill, Matlock, Derbyshire, built 1783. The centre bays of this cotton mill with three-light Venetian windows and a cupola over a stairwell lit by segmental windows, mark the offices for receiving customers.

can be called architecture. The majority of other factories at the time were solid rectangular blocks with symmetrical façades and plain window surrounds; occasionally, the building was graced with a triangular pediment. The vastness of the early spinning mills and factories was something their builders never came to terms with; but in the smaller buildings, there was a pretence that it was not industrial but domestic activity hidden behind the walls. The Boundary Works, Longton, Staffordshire, built 1819 in the style of a comfortable Georgian house, is typical of the pottery works of the early nineteenth century. While the huge and impressive West India Docks, London (1802-3) bow to classical architecture with shallow-arched window architraves, they could never be mistaken for dwellings. Later buildings, such as the warehouse at Nos 65-73 James Street, Glasgow (c.1848), not designed to contain vast quantities of merchandise managed to present an elegant classical façade. The Globe Works, Sheffield, was built c.1825 in the current fashion of the Greek Revival.

Boundary Works, King Street, Longton, Staffordshire, built 1819, has the facade of a substantial town house disguising the industry within. This is typical of early nineteenth-century Staffordshire pottery architecture

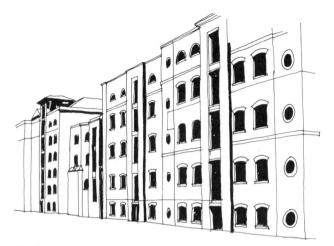

Warehouses in the north half of West India Docks, London, showing two of six blocks linked by lower connecting buildings. String courses and segmental windows are statements of Classical style. Built 1802-3 by George Gwilt.

A late Palladian Revival facade on a general merchandise warehouse of c.1848 at 65-73 James Street, Glasgow. Pre-eminently Classical this demonstrates the conservative Glasgow taste.

The Globe Works, Sheffield, built c.1825. An elegant example of Greek Revival disguising a factory making saws, files and other edge tools.

The impressive booking hall of Curzon Street Station, Birmingham, designed in Greek Ionic by Philip Hardwick in 1838.

The early entrepreneurs were not in direct contact with the public but sold spun yarn to framework knitters who, in turn, sold finished hose to the public. The spinners were remote from the end-user and consequently a factory was not thought of as an advertisement. That conception came in in the second half of the nineteenth century. The new railway companies, anxious to attract travellers, realized the advantage of good architecture. Such impressive station entrances as those of Curzon Street, Birmingham, in the Greek Ionic order by Philip Hardwick (1838), Euston, London, in the Greek Doric, also by Hardwick (1836-9, demolished 1962) and Newcastle-

on-Tyne, in Roman Doric by J. Dobson (1848-63), were deliberately designed to reassure the most timid passenger. Another early attempt at public relations was that at Warwick Gasworks, Saltisford, Warwickshire, built about 1822, where the gas holders are disguised as picturesque Gothic lodges to pacify neighbouring customers living in fear of explosions.

Factories needed high chimneys and they could not be disguised as a domestic accessory. At Chipping Norton, the familiar landmark of the Bliss Tweed Mill of 1872 has all the appearance of a stately home – in a mildly Jacobean style – dropped into the Oxford countryside were it not for a massive Tuscan chimney spoiling the effect. The building is now (1991) being converted into flats. Not all factory chimneys were treated so insensitively. In the mid-nineteenth century Venetian Gothic phase, tall chimneys were disguised as Venetian campaniles. A new mill at Saltaire, Yorkshire, built in 1868 had a chimney copied from the bell-tower of the Santa Maria Gloriosa dei Frari, Venice, alongside a simpler Italianate version already standing on the original 1853 factory. Lister's Manningham Mill, Bradford, built in 1873 has a 250ft-high campanile chimney.

The Warwick Gas Works, Saltisford, Warwickshire. Built c.1822 in the then currently popular Gothick style; the lodges conceal the gas-holders.

In Manchester, the builders of the wholesale warehouses had realized the advertising value of architecture by the mid-century. S. & J. Watts Warehouse in Portland Street is in the Italianate style by Travis and Mangnall in 1851. At No. 103 Princess Street is a much smaller brick palazzo built in 1854 by J.E. Gregan. Still in the same decade, in the Lace Market, Nottingham, Adam's huge lace factory was built in the Jacobean Revival style in 1854-5 by a local architect, T.C. Hine, who managed to make even his domestic commissions look like lace factories. The Temple Mills, Leeds, built 1838-40 by Joseph Bonomi junior is outstanding for the Egyptian style (Bonomi had spent ten years in Egypt).

Six bays of the vast twenty-seven bay length of S. & J. Watts wholesale warehouses in Portland Street, Manchester, built 1855 by Travis and Magnall in the Italianate style to impress customers.

Adam's lace factory, Nottingham Lace Market, built 1854-5 by T.C. Hine in Jacobean style, might be mistaken for a large country house. Daily prayers were said in an underground chapel.

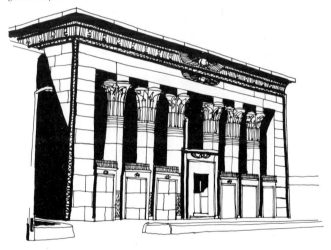

Temple Mills, Leeds. An amazing example of pure Egyptian Revival, built 1838-40 by Bonomi for an eccentric linen manufacturer who grazed a flock of sheep on its grass-covered roof.

One of the unexpected delights of Glasgow is Templeton's Carpet Factory, built in 1889 by W. Leiper in Italian polychromatic Gothic rivalling the Doges' Palace. The city warehouses at No. 81 Miller Street, also in Glasgow, by James Salmon (1849-50) are in a modified Palladian style and that tells us something of the conservatism of Scottish architecture – although No. 37, by Alexander Kirkland (1854) is in an exciting Venetian Renaissance style.

Templeton's Carpet Factory, Glasgow, in high Venetian Gothick by W. Leiper. This extravagant competitor to the Doge's Palace, in red, green and blue brick, could not fail to impress customers.

In their search for economy factory builders developed a fire-resistant construction in the late eighteenth century. It consisted of iron columns supporting brick arching held on cast iron girders. This technique came into common use for industrial buildings only in the 1870s, although it had been used for domestic buildings as early as 1836 at Heath House, Staffordshire, built for a Manchester textile family. From this invention it seems but a short step to steel-framed construction; but it was a long time coming to Britain. Owing to local building regulations external walls were required to be of a minimum thickness, a regulation that was not repealed by the London County Council until 1909 and then only if steel-framed construction were employed. The method had been used in France as early as 1871 and in America in 1883. The Ritz Hotel, London (1903-6) by Mewès and Davis in the Louis XVI style, was the first steel-framed building in London. India House, a warehouse in Whitworth Street, Manchester, in vigorous Baroque, is another early steel-framed building of 1905-6.

The high office block had to wait for the invention of a reliable lift. Until then six floors (as, for example, at S. & J. Watts Warehouse) were the maximum believed possible for unfit commercial gentlemen to climb without provoking a heart attack. Hydraulic hoists had been used since the 1840s but it took time for passenger lifts to become practical. An early example of 1860 at the Westminster Hotel, London, never worked properly; but by the 1880s lifts were becoming more reliable and higher office blocks possible.

THE MODERN ERA

The Modernist Trend 1900-80

Although the 'Battle of the Styles' was over long before the end of the nineteenth century, concluding in defeat for both classical and Gothic by the cosy Domestic Revival, the classical style never went away. The early years of the new century saw fashions for the Edwardian Baroque such as in the Country Life offices, London, W.C.2., by Lutyens of 1904, and the luxurious French styles of Mewès and Davis as demonstrated in the Ritz Hotel, Piccadilly, W.1.

The Country Life Offices, Tavistock Street, London, was, in 1904, Lutyens' first London building. This Edwardian Baroque later evolved into his 'Wrennaissance' domestic style

Banks, playing safe, invariably settled for impressive classical columns. Lutyens invented a 'Wrenaissance' style which perversely, and historically incorrect, followed the Edwardian Baroque

The exception to the general decline in Gothic was church building, where the style was almost universal. Sir Ninian Comper had a wholly ecclesiastical practice and many churches of the first half of the twentieth century are his. St Mary's, Wellingborough, Northamptonshire, of 1908-30 and in a Perpendicular style, has spectacular fan vaulting in the nave and is said to be his favourite church. More generally known is his St Cyprian's, Clarence Gate, N.W.1 of 1903.

The nave of St Mary's, Wellingborough, Northamptonshire, built 1908-30 by Sir Ninian Comper in the late Perpendicular style, is his most complete and best work.

In the years immediately preceding World War I 'Art Nouveau' became fashionable. The style is principally one of decoration and some of the Arts and Crafts work of Burne-Jones in the 1880s displays the sinuous elongated and exotic curves of the Art Nouveau style. In Britain anything so exotic must have been inspired in France, hence the French name given to it. It was, however, developed in Belgium by Victor Horta in 1893-1903. The Scottish architect, Charles Rennie Mackintosh, using Voysey's style and developing brilliant designs of his own, was the real force behind the style in Britain. It is still difficult to realize that Mackintosh's Glasgow School of Art of 1898-9 is almost a hundred years old.

The Glasgow School of Art, built 1898-9 by Mackintosh in a distinctive Art Nouveau style is, unbelievably, nearly 100 years old.

The outstanding architect of the first half of the twentieth century was Sir Edwin Lutyens, who developed the Domestic Revival to lengths undreamed of by Philip Webb. He was also happy with classical motifs, used with amazing results in an Anglo-Indian style in the Viceroy's House (1913-31), New Delhi, India.

The Modern Movement in architecture arrived in Britain in the late 1920s. 'Modernism' rejected ornament and expressed the importance of structure in exploiting the new methods of construction. Many of the architects involved were foreign or born in the Dominions: Serge Chermayeff (1900-) from the Caucasus, who built the De la Warr Pavilion at Bexhill in 1934-5 with his partner Erich Mendelsohn who left Germany in 1933; Erno Goldfinger (1900-) from Hungary; Walter Gropius (1883-1969), arrived from Germany in 1934 and was responsible, with his English partner, Maxwell Fry, for the Impington Village School, Cambridgeshire, in 1934-5; Wells Coates (1893-1958), a Canadian, who with Chermayeff, the New Zealander McGrath (1903-), and others contributed to the interior of Broadcasting House in the 1930s and unfortunately removed by the BBC.

The standard of design of private housing between the wars was depressing. The speculative builder, who had first appeared in the late eighteenth century, erected street after street of two and three bedroom suburban houses in styles demanded by a public dreaming of a non-existent rural past. Mock Tudor fronts tricked out with false half-timbering and bay-windows with leaded lights were standard products. This style had descended from the Arts and Crafts movement through the Vernacular Revival to the cheapest end of the market, stripped bare of all original meaning.

Patrons of architecture after World War II were seldom private clients. More usually they were commercial enterprises building factories, warehouses and office blocks, either as their own headquarters or for letting, or local government authorities or the central government. Their aim, with few exceptions, was to provide the maximum floorspace at the lowest cost. Good architecture was hardly considered and the contribution a building made to its surroundings was not taken into account. Architects' drawings showed buildings in isolation and not as part of a group. The result was that old, good buildings were replaced by featureless panel-clad rectangles of no architectural merit that added a depressing character to the street scene. Post World War II commercial patrons had forgotten that good architecture is good advertising. The pioneering of new building techniques and exploitation of steel-framed and reinforced concrete structures, moreover, resulted in the rejection of the old, tried classical rules of proportion and the principles of Gothic engineering worked out for stone construction. In Britain, no alternative creed for the new materials replaced the trusted and tried principles of centuries. In Britain this passed for Modernism.

Abroad, some good architecture was built but in Britain the lessons mainly went unlearned. Two notable exceptions are the Economist Building, 25 St James's Street, S.W.1., built by Alison and Peter

Smithson in 1964 with the objective, unusual for the 1960s, of making a modern building compatible with the eighteenth-century scale of its neighbours. Although composed of slender concrete uprights, giving the building a strong vertical emphasis concluding with a stumpy roof line, it does not quarrel with the horizontal line of the elegant Adam-type, Boodle's Club with which it rubs shoulders. It is rare for so modern a building to be listed by the DoE but this one is. It is even rarer for a building to be listed when only twenty-five years old, but the Willis Faber Building at Ipswich built by Foster Associates in 1975 has recently been listed as a building of architectural interest. The building on three floors is a sheer wall of rippling glass filled with Baroque movement, whose floors appear to float effortlessly on the air. This is a direct descendant of Sir William Owen's Boots factory and is one of the few modern buildings to bring gasps of admiration.

By the 1980s, however, there was some sign that the design disasters of the 1960s had been digested. The Lloyd's building in London by Richard Rogers, opened in 1989, accepts several of the old principles. There is no pretence about the building; it is asymmetrical and the steel-framed construction is not disguised, so meeting two Gothic criteria. Inside, the vast, high atrium with colonnaded rooms off it harks back to Roman atria and thus meets something of the old classical formulae. Some report that the building is difficult to work in; that is the antithesis of Gothic planning, rediscovered by the Arts and Crafts movement. The cleaning down and maintenance of the exterior stainless steel cladding is constant and will become increasing costly. It remains for posterity to decide whether it is good architecture; it is certainly striking architecture.

Some good architecture and some bad has been created at the Universities of Oxford and Cambridge by patrons not driven by the profit motive. The chapel of Churchill College, Cambridge, begun in 1959 by Richard Sheppard, Robson and Partners in the modernist style, could make a claim to be derived from the classical in that the building is symmetrical about an axis and, in the Adam manner, its assertive exterior is contrasted by an interior of peace and harmony. St Catherine's College, Oxford, begun by Arne Jacobsen in 1960, is outstanding architecture in a decade of downright bad work. Consistent in plan and with meticulous attention to detail, it has yet to be bettered in this century.

INDUSTRIAL ARCHITECTURE

The advertising advantage of having a good building by a good architect was realized by the end of the century. Voysey's small wallpaper factory at Turnham Green, London (1902-3) for Sanderson's for whom he designed wallpaper, is in no style but Voysey's. The Charterhouse Cold Storage warehouse in Smithfield, London, was built in 1900 in the Wren style and is by Arthur Macmurdo, an Arts and Crafts contemporary of Voysey. The one-off Michelin House in Fulham Road, London, S.W.3., built in the Art

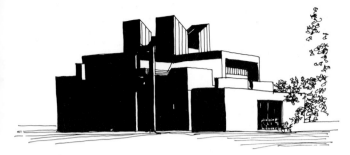

Churchill College chapel, Cambridge, was built 1959 by Richard Sheppard, Dobson & Partners. Although Symmetrical about an axis, as in Classical architecture, the interior with central altar, is Byzantine.

Sanderson's wallpaper factory, Turnham Green, London, built 1902-3 is one of Voysey's few non-domestic buildings. Voysey designed wallpapers for Sandersons.

Nouveau style by a French architect, F. Espinasse, in 1905-11, celebrates the early history of motoring and was good advertising.

The dawn of the Modern Movement after World War I brought changes. The architectural term Expressionism was used to describe factories devoid of decoration that simply expressed their function and it marked the beginning of the Modern Movement. The style was pioneered as early as 1909 in Germany. Expressionism only influenced commercial architecture in Britain in the 1930s. The leading Expressionist architect was Sir Owen Williams (1890-1969) and the Daily Express building, Fleet Street, London, of 1932-9, and the Empire Swimming Pool, Wembley, of 1934, show his talent. The

Opposite: The Charterhouse Cold Storage Co., at Smithfield, London, commissioned Mackmurdo in 1900 to design a Wren Baroque facade, then in the mainstream of fashion.

Below: The Daily Express *building, Fleet Street, London, built 1932 by Clarke & Atkinson with Sir Owen Williams, has a facade in black and clear glass with some impressive Art Deco interiors.*

Boots 'glass' factory at Beeston, Nottingham, is also by Williams and is as admirable today as when built in 1930-2.

Finally, the Art Deco style, taking its name from the Paris Exhibition of 1925, is represented by the Hoover factory on Western Avenue, London, by Wallis Gilbert and Partners, opened in 1932, and the Coty factory on the Great West Road, Heston, by the same firm and completed a year later. These stand on busy main roads and were deliberately designed to catch the eye of the growing motoring public. By then another principle emerged: the more striking the architecture the better the advertising.

Boots' Factory, Beeston, Nottingham. Expressionism by Sir Owen Williams in 1930-2 – the processes within are clearly expressed through the all-glass facades.

The Hoover Factory on Western Avenue, London, in Art Deco by Wallis Gilbert and Partners 1931-2, could never be missed by the new motoring public.

Some Architects of the Period

Sir Ninian Comper (1864-1960): As a pupil in Bodley's office he acquired a lifelong devotion to a scholarly Gothic style. His practice was completely ecclesiastical and specialized in the Gothic style. He brought exquisite colour work to the Lady chapel of St Barnabas, Pimlico, to the reredos of St Clement, Eastcheap and to the tombs in Southwark Cathedral. He designed St George's chapel, Westminster Abbey, in 1925 and was responsible for many sympathetic church restorations.

Charles Rennie Mackintosh (1868-1928): Brilliant Scottish pioneer of modern design and the British Art Nouveau style. His best known works are the Glasgow School of Art building (1898-9), Hill House, Helensburgh (1902-3), and Mrs Cranston's tea-rooms in Buchanan Street, Glasgow (1897). Mackintosh was ahead of his time and World War I effectively killed his architectural practice. Examples of his work are few but influential, and after many years of neglect his genius is at last appreciated.

St Catherine's College, Oxford, built 1960-4 by Arne Jacobson. Consistent in plan, with Classical purity and calm, this is one of the great buildings of the century.

Sir Edwin Lutyens (1869-1944): In 1887 Lutyens entered the office of Ernest George and Peto where he assimilated the Domestic Revival styles of the practice. He also encountered Norman Shaw, who became his lifelong hero, and was influenced by Philip Webb's work. Lutyens, sharing to the full in the grandeur of the Imperial Edwardian years, was the ideal architect for the last of the spectacular English country houses. Lindisfarne Castle, Holy Island, Northumberland (1903), the romantic restoration of a Tudor castle, Castle Drogo, Devon, an amazing twentieth-century castle project (1910-30), and the neo-Georgian Great Maytham, Kent (1907-9), demonstrate Lutyens's versatility. He was a brilliant master of composition and balance, two essentials of good architecture overlooked by the majority of modern architects. However, his Grosvenor estate buildings in Marsham Street, Westminster, are as bad as any of the International Modern school.

Sir Owen Williams (1890-1969): An engineer who practised as a largely self-taught architect. He pioneered the use of reinforced concrete in his large-scale constructions. He also introduced Expressionism, the beginning of 'modernist' architecture. Unconsciously, he was returning to the principles of Pugin, Ruskin and Morris: a building should not pretend to be what it is not. There is, for example, no doubt what his glass and reinforced concrete Boots factory, Beeston, Nottingham (1930-2), was intended for: the activities within are expressed, or shown, through the glass.

Sir Basil Spence (1907-76): Worked with Lutyens whose influence is evident in his buildings. He was one of the few modern British architects who could manage the monumental style. In the inter-war period Spence designed some large private houses in Scotland; but he is best known for Coventry Cathedral, completed in 1960, and Sussex University from 1960. The much criticized Knightsbridge Barracks, Hyde Park S.W.1. (1967-9) contributes nothing to either Park or street.

Hill House, Helensburgh, Strathclyde Region. Mackintosh's finest house built 1902-4. The interior with much white painted woodwork is Art Nouveau at its best.

Castle Drogo, Devonshire. A rich man's medieval fantasy realised by Lutyens in 1910-30. Massive and uncompromising, dramatic use is made of light and shadow, space, and asymmetrical placing of the windows.

Where to See Examples

London – ***British Medical Association*** (B.M.A.HQ.) Burton Street, classical façade by Lutyens 1911-13, WC1; ***Country Life Offices***, Lutyens's first London office block, in 'Wrenaissance' style 1904, Tavistock Street WC2; ***Daily Express Building***, Expressionism by Sir Owen Williams 1932-9, Fleet Street EC4; **Economist Building,** St James's Street, SW1., Alison & Peter Smithson 1964; ***Empire Swimming Pool***, Expressionism by Sir Owen Williams 1934, Wembley; ***Hampstead Garden Suburb***, St Jude-on-the-Hill, the Free Church and the Institute all in the neo-Georgian heart of the suburb by Lutyens 1910 and 1933, NW11; ***Knightsbridge Barracks***, an unworthy tower and building by Basil Spence 1967-9, SW1; ***Lutyens House***, neo-classical by Lutyens 1924-7, Moorgate, EC2.

North – ***Lindisfarne Castle*** (NT), Holy Island, Northumberland, restoration of a Tudor castle by Lutyens in 1903; ***Liverpool***, R.C. Cathedral of Christ the King, in a mixture of classical and Byzantine styles unfinished by Lutyens 1929-40.

Midlands – ***Boots Factory***, Beeston, Nottingham, Expressionism in glass and concrete by Sir Owen Williams 1930-2; ***Luton Hoo*** (The Werner Family), Bedfordshire, remodelled in French Ritz style by Charles Mewès 1904-5; ***Oxford***, St Catherine's College, by Aren Jacobsen begun 1960; ***Renishaw Gardens*** (Sir R. Sitwell), Derbyshire, Italian garden created by Sir George Sitwell between 1900 and 1930s.

East – ***Cambridge***, Churchill College chapel by Richard Sheppard, Robson and Partners begun 1959.

South – ***Great Maytham Hall*** (Co. Hos. Ass. Ltd.), Kent, neo-Georgian by Lutyens 1907-9; ***Polesden Lacey*** (NT), Surrey, remodelled and enlarged by Ambrose Poynter 1906; ***Port Lympne*** (Mr J. Aspinall), Kent, brick Cape Dutch style by Herbert Baker 1918-21; ***Sussex University***, Sussex, Sir Basil Spence from 1960; ***Sissinghurst***

Castle (NT), Kent, a remarkable garden created by Nigel Nicholson and his wife Vita Sackville West in the 1930s.

South-West – *Castle Drogo* (NT), Devon, a twentieth-century castle by Lutyens 1910-30; *Hestercombe* (Somerset C.C. Fire Brigade HQ.), Somerset, orangery and multi-level garden by Lutyens with Gertrude Jekyll 1904.

Scotland – *The Hill House* (NTS), Helensburgh, Strathclyde Region, Art Nouveau villa by C.R. Mackintosh 1902-4; *Manderston* (Mr A. Palmer), Borders Region, large and neo-Classical by John Kinross 1894-1905.

SUGGESTIONS FOR FURTHER READING

GENERAL

Architecture: Nineteenth and Twentieth Centuries by Henry-Russell Hitchcock; Pelican History of Art series, Penguin Books, 1958

Architecture in Britain 1530-1830 by John Summerson; Pelican History of Art series, Penguin Books, 1970.

The Buildings of England, originally by Nikolaus Pevsner, subsequently revised by others. A county by county series of about 50 volumes, published by Penguin. The series has now been supplemented by *The Buildings of Scotland* and *The Buildings of Wales*.

The Pattern of English Building by Alec Clifton-Taylor; Faber & Faber, 1972.

ECCLESIASTICAL

Cathedrals and Abbeys of England & Wales by Richard Morris; Dent, 1979.

Parish Churches by Hugh Braun; Faber & Faber, 1974.

Medieval Monasteries of Great Britain by L. Butler & C. Given-Wilson; Michael Joseph, 1983.

Our Christian Heritage by W. Rodwell & J. Bentley; Guild Publishing, 1984.

HOUSES

A History of the English House by Nathaniel Lloyd; reprint by Omega Books, 1985.

The History of the English House by Alfred Gotch; reprint by Bracken Books, 1985.

The Victorian Country House by Mark Girouard; Yale University Press, 1979.

Victorian Architecture in Britain, Blue Guide series, by Julian Orbach; A. & C. Black (Publishers), Ltd.

The Traditional Buildings of England, by Anthony Quiney; Thames & Hudson, 1990.

The Smaller English House by Lyndon F. Cave; Robert Hale, 1985.

Vernacular Architecture by R.W. Brunskill; Faber & Faber, 1988.

Sweetness & Light by Mark Girouard; Yale University Press, 1977.

CASTLES

Castles by Plantagenet Somerset Fry; David & Charles, 1980.
The National Trust Book of British Castles by Paul Johnson; Weidenfeld & Nicholson, 1978.

ORGANIZATIONS CONCERNED WITH THE CARE OF HISTORIC BUILDINGS

English Heritage, Fortress House, Savile Row, London, W1X 1AB.
Historic Buildings & Monuments of Scotland, PO Box 157, Edinburgh, EH3 7QD.
Heritage in Wales, Dept. EH, Cadw, Brunel House, 2 Fitzalan Road, Cardiff, CF2 1UY.

Ancient Monuments Society, St Andrew-by-the-Wardrobe, Queen Victoria Street, London, EWC4V 5DE.
Friends of Scottish Monuments, Historic Scotland, SDD Room 306, 20 Brandon Street, Edinburgh, EH3 5RA.
The Georgian Group, 37 Spital Square, London, W1R 6AB.
Historic Houses Association, 2 Chester Street, London, SW1X 7BB.
The National Trust, 36 Queen Anne's Gate, London, SW1H 9AS.
The National Trust for Scotland, 5 Charlotte Square, Edinburgh, EH2 4DU.
The Society for the Protection of Ancient Buildings, 37 Spital Square, London, W1R 6AB.
Society of Architectural Historians of Great Britain, Hon. Secretary, Ms. Sally Jeffery, 23b Home Park Road, Wimbledon, London, SW19.
Alexander Thomson Society, 1 Moray Place, Strathbungo, Glasgow, G41 2AQ.
Thirties Society, 58 Crescent Lane, London, SW4 9PV.
The Victorian Society of Great Britain, 1 Priory Gardens, Bedford Park, London, W4 1TT.

Many counties have their own building preservation societies.

Index